Spiritual Counsels of Father John of Kronstadt

Select Passages from *My Life in Christ*
edited and introduced by

W. JARDINE GRISBROOKE

James Clarke & Co
Cambridge

St. Vladimir's Seminary Press
Crestwood, N.Y.

First published 1967

© W. Jardine Grisbrooke

Reprinted 1981

ISBN 0 227 67856 7

Published by:

**James Clarke & Co
7 All Saints' Passage
Cambridge CB2 3LS
England**

**St. Vladimir's Seminary Press
Crestwood
N.Y. 10707
U.S.A.**

Printed in Great Britain by
Redwood Burn Ltd., Trowbridge, Wiltshire, and
bound by Pegasus Bookbinding, Melksham, Wiltshire.

CONTENTS

Introduction

The nineteenth century was in Russia a time of considerable religious revival, and one of the most notable features of this revival was the way in which many thousands of ordinary people, of all classes and callings, flocked for spiritual advice—and, indeed, for temporal advice also—to elders or *startsi,* who exercised in this way a remarkable ministry. But whereas the *startsi*—among whom special mention must be made of the greatest of them all, Saint Seraphim of Sarov,[1] and the several great spiritual directors of the monastery of Optino—were all monks, the last of the famous spiritual teachers of imperial Russia was a married parish priest. On the eve of the revolutionary upheaval, in which the Russian Church was to be tried in the fires of a persecution unequalled in extent or fury by anything the church had suffered in sixteen centuries, it was no monk, but the 'ordinary' priest of an 'ordinary' parish, no elder in some sheltered conventional retreat, but a man who had to find Christ in the rush and bustle—and the squalor and misery—of a great seaport, whom God sent as a sign to his children, to strengthen them for the horrors to come. And the teaching reflects the man and his circumstances—it is as down to earth, yet as caught up to heaven, as the man himself: intensely practical, intensely demanding—and, inescapably, possible for all.

John Ilyitch Sergieff, the son of poor peasant folk, was born on 19 October, 1829 at the little village of Soura, in the

[1] Born 1759, died 1833, canonised 1903.

xi

province of Arkhangelsk in the far north of Russia.[2] The beauty of the natural environment of his early life—for Soura was situated amid majestic scenery—greatly impressed the boy, and throughout his life he was acutely aware of the spiritual witness of the material world to its Creator.

His parents, poor and simple though they were, took great pains over his education, both spiritual and temporal. From the first he displayed understanding of, and love for, the services of the church; but his intellectual formation was longer delayed, for he had great difficulty in learning to read—he himself tells us that he could still read only block capitals when at the age of nine he was sent to school in Arkhangelsk. Still making little headway, and grieving bitterly at it, for he knew how difficult it was for his parents to find the money for his education, he prayed earnestly for divine enlightenment, and one morning, after he had risen during the night and prayed while his companions slept, he found himself able to read easily, and to understand what he had read.

From school, passing out top of his year, he went to seminary, and thence, once more first of his year, he was sent, in 1851, at the cost of the government, to the Theological Academy of Saint Petersburg. While he was there his father died, and it was with great thankfulness to God that he accepted the post of registrar—offered to him on account of his perfect handwriting—and was able to send his little honorarium of ten roubles a month to his mother.

Having considered becoming a monk, and going to eastern Siberia as a missionary, he came to the conclusion that there were many people around him as unenlightened as any pagan, and he decided to work for their salvation, after a dream in answer to prayer, in which he saw himself officiating in some unknown cathedral.

---

[2] Typically, in the midst of his amazingly full life, Father John never forgot Soura: he visited it every year, and bestowed many gifts upon it, among them a new church and a school.

Soon after completing his studies he married Elisabeth, daughter of the Archpriest K. P. Nevitzki, and he was ordained priest on 12 December, 1855. Appointed assistant priest at Saint Andrew's Cathedral, Kronstadt, as he entered it for the first time he recognised the church he had seen in his dream; and there, first as curate, and afterwards as rector, he served throughout the fifty-three years of his ministry. Cherishing a lofty ideal of the priestly vocation, he continued at night to study and to pray, that he might perfect himself in it, while during the day he devoted himself to the many poor of his parish.

The inhabitants of Kronstadt, a naval base situated on an island at the mouth of the Neva, not far from Saint Petersburg, were in 1855 drawn largely from the very worst elements of the population of the capital, and much of the place was a festering sore of sin and filth, of poverty and misery, of disease and starvation. Father John, whose predecessors, apparently, had hardly even dared to penetrate the worst parts of the town, spent much of his time there, striving to heal bodies and souls alike, attracting to himself first the children, and then, through them, their parents. Often he found no time to eat until the late evening, and even then he would sometimes be summoned out again, and not return before the small hours; he gave away his own shoes, he gave away the housekeeping money: his wife gradually accustomed herself to it, and finally became something like his keeper.

He lived in a barely furnished cottage on the seaboard, whence he was soon unable to emerge without being attended by a crowd, which would wait at the door of his house, or of the cathedral, and follow him through the streets. Early each morning, after a period of intense prayer before an icon at home, he would go to church—as usual, through a crowd—and there sing the liturgy in a deep, clear and powerful voice: for normally he celebrated the eucharist—or at least communicated—every day. Afterwards he would pay twelve or fifteen sick calls, fulfil teaching engagements, and often go into Saint Petersburg for similar purposes, for his renown as a powerful intercessor and healer grew very rapidly, and spread throughout the country. Every moment he received appeals for spiritual and material assistance, and never was such an appeal unanswered; daily he received scores of visitors, and hundreds of letters, while the crowds pressed round him wherever he appeared—in the streets of Kronstadt or Saint Petersburg, at the railway stations, everywhere. In summer he would talk with the poor in the fields outside the town, sitting on the grass, with the children by him, and the adults standing or sitting around. Rich and poor, he was ready to help all, and he treated all alike—often some important personage, with whom he had an appointment, had to wait for a Father John delayed by answering the urgent appeals of poor folk in the crowds. It is not surprising to learn that he habitually walked fast!

In 1857 he was invited to teach scripture in the municipal school at Kronstadt, and he accepted with joy, for he loved children, and always took great pains with them. He was much loved in return by his pupils—some delightful anecdotes survive on this score, which unfortunately we have not the space to reproduce—and on this he based his authority; he never needed to use either severity or mockery. The bible, he held, should not be taught just like any other subject, but with faith and love, to awaken faith and love in others, and the measure of his own success may be estimated from the fact that, while he never insisted that his pupils must go to church, they all went when he celebrated. When his fame spread, and he had constantly to visit Saint Petersburg, he had, to his own, and his colleagues' and pupils', great regret, to abandon his teaching post.

Another object of Father John's concern and labour was the

removal of the vast amount of mendicancy with which Kronstadt was afflicted. At first he gave these beggars money for food and shelter, but he soon came to see that this was not merely useless, but positively harmful. In 1868 he conceived the idea of founding a House of Industry, comprising a number of workshops, a dormitory, a refectory, a dispensary, and a primary school. He formed a committee, and appealed for funds. His appeal was answered by rich and poor from all over Russia, and the House of Industry was founded in 1873. Father John administered a total of over £15,000 a year in numerous charities, one half of it in Kronstadt.

How did he manage to do it all? He had the ability—acquired, no doubt, by prayer and patience—to snatch a short period of deep sleep wherever and whenever he got the chance; and he had a great love of the early morning hours for prayer and meditation—but his early morning walks in his garden were soon discovered, and then farewell to solitude! Often, indeed, he could barely save half-an-hour for his own prayers. On the rare occasions when he was able to pass a whole day in Kronstadt he liked to walk in the streets towards midnight, praying and meditating: if he saw a light, however, he would knock—often to comfort someone ill or dying, but just as ready to join in laughter and cheerful conversation, if that should be what he found. It is not surprising that he had moments of depression through sheer fatigue; he had been attacked in the same way in his student days, and then and later he overcame them, as he overcame all, as he achieved all, by prayer and, above all, by devout reception of the holy communion.

He himself declared that only by partaking of the Body and Blood of Christ every day was he enabled to accomplish a task otherwise beyond human powers. When he came to partake of the blessed sacrament he would be utterly transfigured —all weariness, all burden of trouble and sorrow gone, and every line of his face reflecting an extraordinary spiritual joy, heavenly peace, and a great feeling of strength and power. Is it any wonder that his church was packed to the doors, Sundays and weekdays alike? The great cathedral of Saint Andrew at Kronstadt could hold seven thousand people, and when Father John celebrated the liturgy it was so crowded that, as the Russian saying has it, 'even an apple could not have found room to fall to the ground'.

Loved alike by rich and poor, by nobleman and beggar, Father John was not, however, *universally* popular. There were those who looked upon him and his works with jealousy and ill-will; particularly among clergy and civil servants there were many who disliked him. On the other hand, towards the end of his life, his absolute conservatism, convinced and outspoken, on matters of principle, both theological and political, aroused the bitter enmity of the 'liberal' pseudo-intellectuals who were zealously preparing the way for the overthrow of both church and monarchy, and with them of every public and private virtue, and the establishment of an ungodly and in-human tyranny. They could not but hate one who saw them for what they were, who preached Christianity so powerfully and persuasively, and whose own life was an example of it far more persuasive than any preaching.

For his part, Father John during his last years constantly predicted the approach of terrible events in Russia, and openly denounced those who with increasing success were leading people astray, above all those in positions of authority. In all his sermons of 1907 he spoke of the terrible judgment of God, and urged the need of repentance and a return to common sense, declaring that if Russia ceased to be *Holy* Russia, she would become nothing more than a mere horde of tribal savages, intent upon destroying each other.

Father John's health began to decline in 1906, and towards the end of 1908 he became very ill, and was unable to get any rest from his sufferings, except during his daily liturgy, which he continued to celebrate as long as possible, doing so for the last time on 10 December. He still communicated daily, but on 18 December he fell into a coma, from which, however, he awoke the following evening, much afflicted in his soul. Having with great difficulty received communion for the last time, he died at twenty minutes to seven on the morning of 20 December.

His body was taken solemnly to Saint Petersburg, and there interred in the great church of the convent of Saint John, which he had founded. The whole route of the procession, from Kronstadt to Oranienbaum, and again from the Baltic station to the convent, was lined by weeping crowds, mourning the loss of their father and intercessor; even the choir of the imperial guard, who sang the requiem, were unable to restrain their tears. At least sixty thousand people attended the funeral.

He who in this life cared so much for his children, and interceded for them so powerfully, has not abandoned them: the stream of healing, both bodily and spiritual, through his prayers, has not ceased to flow. During the few years between his death and the catastrophe which he foretold, pilgrims journeyed to his tomb, and although, in the circumstances which have beset the Russian Church since 1917, it has so far been impossible formally to canonise him inside Russia, since this introduction was first written this final seal of the Church's approval has been set on the devotion of the faithful to him by the synod of the Russian Orthodox Church in Exile, on 1 November, 1964.

Those who have written about Father John are by no means all agreed upon his place in the history of Russian Orthodox spirituality; of his importance, his significance, there can be no question, but there are widely divergent views as to wherein that importance and significance actually lie. To take but two

xvii

examples, Professor Fedotov maintains that he 'deviates sharply from the main pattern of Russian sanctity',[3] while Professor Meyendorff clearly regards him as fitting within it.[4] I do not think that either verdict can be maintained without qualification.

In the first place, it is important to realise that the Russian spiritual tradition from the sixteenth century onward was deeply divided; there were in fact two traditions, not one. This is not the place to recount the story of the division, which can be read elsewhere;[5] it must suffice to outline only those salient points of it which had survived or developed by the second half of the nineteenth century. The tradition represented in the sixteenth century by the party of Saint Joseph of Volokolamsk was by the nineteenth century in a sorry state. It had suffered a severe blow in the Old Believer schism of the seventeenth century, which from then on deprived the established church of the most devout and most zealous—if, indeed, the most fanatical—of the adherents of that tradition. As a result it was by this time hardly a living spiritual tradition at all; teaching and practice alike were formalist and decadent, and it wielded little spiritual—as distinct from ecclesiastical— influence. Clearly one would not expect Father John to owe much to it. Yet as a matter of fact in one respect at least Father John's teaching is closer to this 'conventional' religion than to that of the other and more flourishing school of spirituality— his emphasis on the importance of liturgical worship, on assiduous attendance at divine service, on respect for, and use of, all the rites of the church; an emphasis in marked contrast with the attitude to such things sometimes—not always—to be

[3] G. P. Fedotov, *A Treasury of Russian Spirituality*, p. 347.

[4] J. Meyendorff, *St. Grégoire Palamas et la Mystique Orthodoxe*, pp. 171–2.

[5] For a convenient short account of the relevant periods of Russian church history, see Timothy Ware, *The Orthodox Church*, ch. 6, *Moscow and St. Petersburg*.

found amongst the adherents of the other tradition, which we may call the 'monastic-mystical' school.[6]

To assess Father John's relationship to the latter—represented in nineteenth-century Russia above all by the *startsi*, although not only by them—is a much more difficult task. It is evidently of this tradition that both Fedotov and Meyendorff were thinking when they came to opposed conclusions; and, as I see it, their divergence is rather in their assessment of the tradition than in their assessment of Father John. Be that as it may, I believe it to be misleading to suggest that Father John owed little or nothing to the monastic-mystical tradition, and equally misleading to assert his dependence upon it without at the same time taking full account of the considerable differences between his life and teaching and those of many of the exponents of that teaching.

The differences are indeed marked. Fedotov's statement that 'Father John was not an ascetic but was content with rejecting the world interiorly and living according to the precepts of the Church'[7] seems to require some qualification, to put it mildly, in the light of Father John's heroic life of good works, unless the word 'ascetic' is to be defined in an intolerably limited sense; but it is true that his asceticism took the form of strict obedience to the Church's rules of fasting and abstinence, for example, and, for the rest, of accepting whatever tribulations and mortifications God sent to him, and required of him, in his remarkable daily life; he did not go out of his way to invent artificial mortifications for himself. Again, as we have seen, he would give away the very shoes from his feet; but, as his photographs bear witness, he did not refuse to wear the rich

[6] Strictly, the Hesychast tradition: but for my present purpose I prefer to use a less technical term, and I believe 'monastic-mystical' conveys quite adequately the fundamental character of this spirituality.

[7] *Op. cit.*, p. 347.

cassocks which admirers pressed upon him, nor the decorations which his sovereigns bestowed upon him: evidently he had no inclination to indulge in any artificial display of humility. Saint and miracle-worker though he was, this priest who so evidently walked with God was no mystic in the conventional sense of the word; and his teaching, from which any suggestion of a method or system of mental prayer, and any elaborate allegories of spiritual ladders, dark nights of the soul, and so forth, are conspicuously absent, was based simply on the bible, rather than upon the *Philokalia,* which played so great a part in the formation of the nineteenth-century monastic-mystical tradition. In all this Father John does diverge sharply, both in his life and in his teaching, from that tradition.

It may be objected, however, that this is a one-sided picture, and that the contrast is overdrawn. It is true that Father John neither taught nor practised any system of mental prayer; but he did, apparently, both use and recommend to others the Jesus Prayer, which was so important an element in the practice of the monastic-mystical tradition. Moreover, this particular contrast is even less marked if one bears in mind that in fact not all the monastic-mystical teachers advocated the physical exercises which commonly accompanied the recitation of the Jesus Prayer: Theophan the Recluse, for example, in his edition of the *Philokalia*, either omits the references to them altogether or else includes a stiff footnote advising the reader not to try them.[8] And it would certainly be unjust to suggest that the bible was ignored, or its importance in any way minimised, in the monastic-mystical tradition. On the contrary, writers in that tradition, in every century, have insisted on the importance of reading the scriptures and laying them to heart.

Nevertheless, although the contrast must not be overdrawn, it does exist. If one makes a careful comparison of Father

---

[8] On the other hand, Saint Nicodemus of the Holy Mountain did recommend their use, and they feature also in *The Way of a Pilgrim*.

John's writing with, for example, that very significant little book *The Way of a Pilgrim*,[9] it is hardly possible not to see the difference. The Pilgrim carries a bible with him wherever he goes, and reads it regularly and devotedly; but his spirituality is not biblical as Father John's is biblical. Take away the bible, and simple teaching based upon it, from *My Life in Christ*, and you have little left; take it away from *The Way of a Pilgrim*, and the loss is not nearly so great. The Pilgrim has a great devotion to the bible, but his spirituality is not primarily and fundamentally biblical, as Father John's is: devotion to the bible does not necessarily imply a truly biblical spirituality, any more than devotion to the reserved sacrament necessarily implies a truly eucharistic spirituality. Again, the theme of intense prayer runs through both of them; but there is a marked difference in the tone of the prayer, in the type of prayer; even in the use of the Jesus Prayer, there is surely a contrast between Father John's simple advice to keep the Holy Name always upon one's lips, and the Pilgrim's use of it as a form repeated twelve thousand times a day. I would not be misunderstood: I do *not* wish to suggest that the one way is right and the other wrong; nor, indeed, that the one is intrinsically better than the other—*In my Father's house are many mansions*. But I *do* wish to suggest that Father John's way is more likely to be spiritually profitable to the majority of ordinary Christian men and women, for whom this book is intended.

What of Father John's convinced and ardent sacramentalism, and in particular his insistence on frequent offering and partaking of the eucharist? It contrasted sharply with the common practice of the day, the sour fruit of what I have called the conventional tradition; did it also contrast with that

[9] English translation by R. M. French, 1954. Concerning this book, see Fedotov, op. cit., pp. 280–2; Meyendorff, op. cit., pp. 169–70; Ware, op. cit., pp. 134, 313–4.

of the monastic-mystical tradition? This is not an easy question to answer, for the latter has varied considerably. The great fourteenth-century Greek exponent and defender of hesychasm, Saint Gregory Palamas, and his close associate Nicholas Cabasilas, were both thoroughly and emphatically sacramentalist; and Cabasilas, moreover, is one of the most noted of Orthodox liturgical writers. Nor was the practice of frequent communion without its witnesses among their eighteenth- and nineteenth-century successors: Saint Nicodemus of the Holy Mountain defended it so ardently that he got himself into trouble with the ecclesiastical authorities; there are plenty of references to the eucharist in the letters of the *startsi* and several of the elders of Optino communicated daily, at certain periods of their life, as did Saint Seraphim. Saint Seraphim, however, displays in his own person the considerable variation to which I have referred. After his ordination as deacon he ministered and communicated daily for a whole year; at another period of his life he went three years together without either receiving communion or going to church; and then, when for this reason his superiors recalled him from his hermitage, he took to receiving communion every Sunday—but still he did not go to church: it was brought to him in his cell, 'in order that there should be no violation of his enclosure and silence'.[10]

In my Father's house are many mansions: let us not presume to criticise so great a saint. But the apparently inconsistent sacramental life which may have been God's will for Saint Seraphim is clearly not a model to be generally imitated with spiritual profit; whereas Father John's firm and consistent teaching and practice clearly are such a model. If the conventional tradition led to a widespread and grave neglect of the sacramental life, the revived monastic-mystical tradition did little to remedy that neglect; and, indeed, it may even

10 Quoted by Fedotov, op. cit., p. 251.

unintentionally have aggravated it, by accidentally distracting attention to other, superficially more fascinating, aspects of the spiritual life. Too many ordinary Orthodox still look upon the sacraments with a regard compounded of casual negligence and devout fear. That within the last half-century this attitude has everywhere been shaken to some extent, and in some places largely eradicated, is probably due in no small measure —particularly insofar as it affects Russian circles—to the teaching and example of Father John of Kronstadt, an 'ordinary' parish priest.

For, to borrow the words of Fedotov, his 'specific role was that of a *praying priest*'.[11] Father Meyendorff points out that the very title of *My Life in Christ* bears deliberate reference to Cabasilas' great work on the sacraments, and that he understood all that he did, all that he achieved, as a manifestation of sacramental grace, fighting evil in all its forms. And what is true of his own life is true also of his teaching: it is marked by a clear insistence on the centrality in the Christian life of ordained means of grace, and it is perhaps this above all else which marks him out as a sure spiritual guide for the ordinary man or woman trying to live the Christian life in the world.

This insistence on giving the sacraments their proper place was Father John's greatest legacy to the Orthodox Church, and to the Russian Church in particular, and it was manifest not only in his teaching, but also in his pastoral practice. I have already remarked upon his daily celebration of the liturgy; he himself said that not to celebrate the liturgy was to him as death. Moreover, in sharp contrast with the prevailing custom of very infrequent communion, he insisted that all who worshipped with him should communicate with him also, and since he could not possibly hear the confessions of the thousands who flocked to his church, he substituted for auricular confes-

11 *Ibid.*, p. 348.

sion a form of public confession, his congregation confessing their sins one to another—a daring innovation which, however, received divine sanction in a vision granted to a layman present one day in the church, of our Lord stretching his hands out over all the people as Father John gave the general absolution. Nor was Father John's insistence on the primacy of the eucharist limited to urging more frequent communion; he was also concerned to arouse his congregation to more active and more intelligent participation in the service, and to this end replaced the great solid icon-screen which largely concealed the altar from the people by a low wall according to primitive custom. He was the first 'liturgical reformer' in the modern Orthodox Church, and his example in this respect is of inestimable importance for the life of the Church in these terrible times which he foretold.

With this emphasis on the importance of the sacraments, and of liturgical worship, Father John naturally combined a great devotion to the priesthood, which found expression in his teaching, and in his life. This it was upon which his great influence rested: he was the ideal priest. He lived a life of heroic good works; he was no advocate of impracticable theories, but one who practised what he preached, loving and serving all, beholding his God in all his children: *Inasmuch as ye have done it unto one of the least of these my brethren, ye have done it unto me*. Moreover, his spiritual life was of a kind to encourage others, for his was no sudden outburst of miraculous forces—his great powers of healing and of spiritual insight were the fruit of years of hard prayer.

Prayer—that was the key. And what prayer! 'He was a genius of prayer and a teacher of prayer. All his works of healing were effected by insistent, assiduous prayer, usually in union with the prayer of his patients and their friends.'[12] His faith in prayer was tremendous. He based this prayer on the

[12] Ibid.

promise of God: *Ask, and ye shall receive*, and on the pledge given in the incarnation—God, he maintained, who has given us a gift so infinitely surpassing any other, will not refuse us the lesser things for which we ask. The dominant quality of his prayer—and this is as evident in his teaching as in the anecdotes of his life—was power. He knew delight in prayer, but he did not seek it; and his prayer was not disinterested— he desperately wanted something, and he asked for it, insistently, forcefully, indeed violently, taking full account of the Lord's words: *The kingdom of heaven suffereth violence, and the violent take it by force.* 'He was simply convinced that God cannot refuse to hear the prayer of insistent petition accompanied by the oblation of self.'[13] And in his writings he constantly refers to answers to prayer, and insists with an absolute conviction that it *is* worth while to act upon our Lord's promise: *Ask, and ye shall receive. Seek, and ye shall find. Knock, and it shall be opened unto you.* Time and again he appeals to experience, confidently—to the experience of the saints, and to the experience of sinners, including his own.

It is clear that this irresistible prayer was the source of the extraordinary powers of healing with which he was endowed, a power manifest in hundreds, perhaps thousands, of cases, a power attested by all sorts and conditions of men. It should be noted that he considered prayer as a normal, not an abnormal, means of healing, that he in no way disparaged medical treatment, and that he taught that one must not require miracles of God without extreme necessity. One who was present with Father John in a sick room records the complete transfiguration which came upon him as he prayed 'with an irresistible force of love for his neighbour', of the illumination of his face, and of the perspiration rolling down it, as also the consciousness of a tremendous access of power, by which he knew his prayer to be answered. His healing

13 Ibid.

power was in no way restricted by distance: he would command a girl paralysed in the feet to rise from her bed and walk, whereupon she did so, and was at once fully recovered; he could also pray when celebrating the liturgy at Kronstadt for two children critically ill five hundred miles away in Moscow, who from that moment began rapidly to recover.

Father John's spiritual insight was no less remarkable than his healing power. We have already seen that he foretold the catastrophe of 1917, and urged his hearers to repent before it was too late; but this was by no means the only instance of prophecy on his part, and some of the others which are recorded are perhaps clearer examples of supernatural vision. It might be argued that any really devout and really perceptive man in the Russia of 1907 could have foretold, had he been prepared to face it, the shadow of disaster looming ahead; but this cannot be said of Father John's telling an astonished agnostic professor of Kazan that he would soon become a priest—the man did in fact became both a priest and a monk—or of the occasion when, after holding an intercessory service in a house for a young girl gravely ill, he refused to present the cross to be kissed—the usual custom on such an occasion—to a certain countess who was present, but insisted on presenting it to the sick girl's English Protestant governess, who was standing a little way off. He had never seen either of them before; but the countess was a woman of irregular life, and the governess afterwards became Orthodox.[14] An even more extraordinary example of this supernatural perception was recounted by a woman widowed at an early age, and left with no support, who was driven to such desperation by the plight of her four children, weeping from cold and hunger, that she

14 I owe this anecdote to a close relative of the child visited on this occasion.

decided to commit suicide, reasoning that if they were orphans somebody would take care of them. After a last fruitless effort to find work, weary, hungry, and utterly despairing, she found herself among a crowd waiting for Father John to emerge from a house. The door opened; he appeared, quickly looked round the crowd, and stretched out his hand to the young widow, giving her a purse full of money. Two days later a home accepted care of two of the children, and soon afterwards she herself found work.

To all in distress, indeed, whether spiritual or material, whether through their own sins, or through no fault of their own, Father John was the living embodiment of the divine compassion, merciful and just. More than one story tells of his rescue of a drunkard—drunkenness was a particular curse of nineteenth-century Russia. For the dying he concerned himself greatly, as, again, more than one anecdote records. He attended the death-bed of the Emperor Alexander III, and his own account of it—too long, unfortunately, to reproduce here—is a notable example of his emphasis on the primacy of the sacraments, and the sacramental foundation of his own powers.

Father John's teaching is above all else practical. Its constant theme is that man is engaged in a spiritual warfare, which it is his business to win. *My Life in Christ* might be called a manual of weapon training for that warfare. Foremost among the weapons are those with which the Church of God provides us—the sacraments and sacramentals. Of the essentially sacramentalist character of Father John's spirituality we have already spoken, and the reader will find much of it for himself in the chapter of the present work entitled *The Help of the Church on Earth*.

But sacraments are not magic, and none has emphasised this more clearly than did Father John. For a man to partake of them fruitfully, he must make himself as fit to do so as he can, by prayer, mortification, and good works. And these in their turn he cannot accomplish without the grace of God: and of that, again, he cannot avail himself without faith, itself a divine gift. Father John realised vividly the utter dependence of man on God, and the utter love of God for man; that man without God can do nothing, and that man with God can do everything, is the keynote of all his teaching, and it is linked with an insistence on the absolute necessity of faith. Faith is the *absolute* prerequisite to all else, the *absolutely* indispensable foundation of all prayer, all good works.

Faith, however, is not something which comes automatically—it has to be prayed for. Prayer, and complete conviction of the efficacy of prayer, was, as we have already remarked, the foundation upon which Father John built his amazingly fruitful and powerful ministry, and it is as pronounced in his teaching as in his life. Two points stand out from his teaching on prayer: the one, that prayer can achieve *everything*; the other, that to do so it must be *real* prayer. Time and again he speaks of the fulfilment of prayer offered wholeheartedly and with faith. His teaching on prayer is abundant, thorough, and eminently practical, as the reader will find in the chapter on *The Difficulty of Prayer*.

Another marked characteristic of Father John's teaching is the vivid realisation of the presence of God, and of the communion of the saints, wherewith it is penetrated, the latter finding expression in invocation of the saints, above all of the Mother of God, and in fervent and constant intercession for both living and departed. But Father John does not allow us to escape with the idea that all one's duty to one's neighbour is fulfilled by praying for him—while this is an important part of it (particularly in the case of enemies), it must be accompanied by the evidence of good works, especially towards those who are poorer than ourselves: it is typical of Father John that he speaks of beggars as God's mercy towards us.

Father John's teaching on sin and repentance is essentially simple, as any worthwhile teaching on the subject must be. It combines a great urge to recognise and repent of sin with encouragement to believe in forgiveness. There is, however, one weapon in the battle with sin upon which Father John places tremendous emphasis: mortification of the flesh, especially by fasting and abstinence. This is indeed a traditional Orthodox emphasis, but it may well come as a surprise to the non-Orthodox reader. If at times he suspects that there is an over-emphasis on it, he would do well to bear in mind both the advocacy of fasting in the gospel, and that precisely as a spiritual *weapon*, and also the particular conditions of nineteenth-century Russia, e.g., the widespread drunkenness. A man's teaching is bound to be influenced by the practical issues he has to face, and Father John's is no exception to the rule. Moreover, the fundamental principle of his teaching on fasting is ascetical, not puritanical.[15]

There are, however, a few passages in *My Life in Christ*— some of which are, and some of which are not, included in this book—which force one to ask whether at times the author does not stray well over the boundary between asceticism and puritanism. There are indubitably some in which the language is imprecise, and equally capable of an orthodox or unorthodox meaning; and there are a very few, on the relationship between the flesh and the spirit, in which the

[15] How far Father John was from puritanism is clear from an anecdote dating from his early years in the priesthood. One day he happened to visit a house where a party was in progress. There were many young people present, and it was clear that dancing had been about to begin, but that the company was now refraining from it on account of the presence of a priest. Father John thereupon smilingly asked them why they were not dancing, adding that one ought to dance when young, and that were it not for his cassock he would join them.

interpretation of 'flesh' seems to be less than Pauline, and the resulting doctrine less than orthodox.

It would be unrealistic, however, to press this criticism, or to allow it to prejudice one against Father John's extremely valuable teaching on mortification. Father John was not a professional theologian, and while he was a pioneer of pastoral liturgical reform, and of a renewed emphasis on the sacramental life of the church, he was in other respects a man of his time. Language of that kind was the common theological currency of the day, as it had been for a very long time, and the patristic revival was yet to come. Moreover, the 'spiritual' writer is by the nature of his task more exposed to the danger of falling into this particular snare than is, say, the dogmatic theologian, and few there are that have not fallen into it. In Father John's case we have only to set against occasional lapses of this kind his tremendous love for the beauty of nature, and acute perception of the divine revelation implicit in it,[16] his vivid grasp of the wondrous mystery of the incarnation, and his marked sacramentalism, to realise that these slight blemishes are in no way of the essence of his thought, but rather the incidental effects of the climate in which he wrote. It must also be borne in mind that *My Life in Christ* is not a polished literary work, but a volume of collected jottings, and in these circumstances it is inevitable that some of the wording should be less than precise. The wonder is that he found time to write it at all. For the same reason I have not attempted to eliminate, or even comment further upon, certain minor inconsistencies, which are bound to occur in a book written over so long a period of time.

What is remarkable is the enduring appositeness of the greater part of it: how much spiritual writing of the last century is of any value or relevance at all today? Here, how-

---

[16] I would emphasise this the more in view of the fact that the many passages on this subject in his writings could not be used in this book.

ever, is a body of teaching of lasting force, based firmly on the bible and the church, practical, simple, unaffected—of inestimable value to the ordinary man or woman trying, however haltingly, to lead a 'life in Christ'. Its author passed from this life to the next on the very eve of the great troubles of our time, troubles which he foretold, and for the end of which, as for the salvation of those who must endure them, he does not cease to pray. *Those who desire to see me shall pass through tribulation and despair.*[17] In such a journey a man may have great comfort of his companions, if he choose them wisely. Not all are helped or encouraged by the same company; but some may find that they could take, under God, no surer guide, no stronger companion, than Father John of Kronstadt.

Father John's principal work, *My Life in Christ,* is a massive volume of some three hundred thousand words, and it has been no simple task to extract from it passages amounting to only a fifth of the total, and yet to preserve the balance of his teaching. On the other hand, the original work is completely disorganised, due to the circumstances in which it was written, and not only is it, inevitably, repetitive, but it is also exceedingly verbose: much of it, after all, was written in the age of the three-volume novel. It was not, therefore, impossible, to produce a very much shorter book which should nevertheless convey adequately the substance of the author's teaching.

The contents of the present volume have been selected and arranged, first, to give a reasonably balanced picture of Father John's teaching, and, second, to provide a useful manual of spiritual advice for the believer of today. On the rare occasions when these aims have clashed, the former has

17 Ep. Barn., vii. 11.

been sacrificed to the latter, as Father John himself would wish.

The arrangement of the present volume is, inevitably, somewhat arbitrary, as the original was without arrangement of any kind: but readers familiar with the volume published in 1899 under the title *Thoughts and Counsels of Father John,* by Cyril Bickersteth and Agnes Illingworth, will perceive a debt which I gratefully acknowledge, although my arrangement is not identical with theirs.

I wish to acknowledge also my indebtedness to all who have helped with this book in any way: the Right Reverend Bishop Jean Kovalevsky; the Right Reverend Bishop Jacobus Akkersdijk; the Very Reverend Archpriest Gabriel Bornand; Sister Maria, of the Dutch Orthodox Community of Saint John the Baptist, the Hague; Mother Magdalina, of the Russian Orthodox Convent of Our Lady of Lesna, Fourqueux, France; Messrs Sheed and Ward, for permission to quote from *A Treasury of Russian Spirituality,* by Professor G. P. Fedotov; Mr. A. D. Millard; the Reverend Dr. K. T. R. Ware; and my wife, for her patient and long-suffering help with the considerable amount of checking involved. A debt of another kind which I owe to the Right Reverend Abbess Elisabeth, of the Russian Orthodox Convent of the Annunciation in London, I have attempted to acknowledge, however inadequately, by dedicating this book to her and her community. Finally, it would be churlish not to add here the name of one of whose interest and encouragement I have been acutely aware throughout my labours—John Ilyitch Sergieff sometime Rector of the Cathedral Church of Saint Andrew in Kronstadt.

W. JARDINE GRISBROOKE

I

THE GROUND OF ALL OUR HOPE

The Approach of God to Man: The Incarnation

If man had not been created according to the image of God, the Lord would not have been incarnate of the most holy Virgin.

The Lord, before his incarnation, let man experience all the bitterness of sin, all his powerlessness to eradicate it; and when all longed for a deliverer, then he appeared, the all-wise and all-powerful healer and helper. When men hungered and thirsted after righteousness as it grew weaker, then the everlasting righteousness came.

This is indeed the miracle of miracles; this reveals the infinite mercy, wisdom, and omnipotence of the Lord towards his creatures, that he himself, the Lord of all, the infinite, the unbounded, was pleased and was able to become man that we might be saved, that *the Word, by whom all things were made, was made flesh and dwelt among us,* living with men, and made like unto man in everything, sin alone excepted.

TWO

The Approach of Man to God: Faith, Hope, Trust

Faith is the key to God's treasury: *All things are possible to him that believeth*. Faith is a spiritual mouth, and the more freely it opens, the more freely may the divine streams enter in. Let it open freely, then, as does your bodily mouth; let not your lips be closed by doubt—if they are, the treasury of God's blessing will be closed to you.

What is faith? Sureness of spiritual truth, of that which is, or of, God. To believe means to be as sure of the reality of the spiritual world as of the material world.

Nothing is impossible to those who believe: lively and unshaken faith can accomplish great miracles in the twinkling of an eye. And even without it miracles are wrought, such as those accomplished in the sacraments; for God's mystery is always accomplished, even when we are lacking in faith, when it is celebrated.

Faith gives rest and joy; unbelief troubles and wounds.

How many say 'I believe in God' without really believing! How many are silent when it is necessary to defend the glory of God and of his saints, which is blasphemed by the children of this world! Some are silent when it is necessary to uphold God's truth, or to put a stop to irreverence or blasphemy.

Men have fallen into unbelief because they have either completely lost the spirit of prayer, or never had it—in short because they do not pray.

Unfortunately our faith is hindered by the short-sightedness of our reason. Faith understands directly whilst reason arrives at the truth by circuitous ways; faith is the means of communication between one spirit and another, whilst reason is the means of communication between the spiritually sensual and the simply material; the first is of the spirit, and the latter of the flesh.

If from time to time we do not stir up the fervour of faith in our heart, eventually faith may become entirely extinct in us. The enemy takes pains to attain this end, which is why we see men who are Christians only in name, while their actions are quite heathen.

The means to confirm and strengthen Christian hope are prayer, especially frequent and sincere prayer, confession of our sins, frequent reading of the Word of God, and, above all, frequent communion of the holy and life-giving sacraments of the Body and Blood of Christ.

If you indeed call God your Father, then trust in him as in the one Father, most merciful, all-powerful, most wise, everloving, ever perfect. Trust in him in respect of the blessings of this temporal life, but above all in respect of the future blessings which shall be granted you in Christ Jesus. But as through the love of the heavenly Father for you you have become the child of God; for you have come forth from him endowed with reason and free-will; so on your part you should make every effort to reach that blessed and eternal heavenly inheritance.

Let that which calms my mind and my heart be committed to writing that I may return to constant peace of heart amidst the cares of life. What is it? It is this saying, full of trust and power: 'The Lord is everything to me'. This is the priceless treasure, which if we possess we can be calm in every estate, rich in poverty, generous and kind to others in the time of wealth, and not losing hope even after having sinned.

The Lord is everything to you, and you must be everything to the Lord. As all your treasure is in your heart and your will, and God asks of you your heart, saying, *My son, give me thine heart*, therefore, in order to fulfil God's perfect will, renounce your own corrupt, wayward, plausible will, and know it not; know only God's will. *Not my will, but thine be done.*

II

THE NECESSITY AND BENEFITS OF PRAYER

The Need of Prayer

Why is it necessary to pray at home, and to attend divine service at church? Well, why is it necessary for you to eat and drink, to take exercise, or to work, every day? In order to support the life of the body and strengthen it. So also it is absolutely necessary to pray in order to support the life of the soul, to strengthen the soul, which is sick with sin, and to cleanse it, just as you employ some kinds of food and drink to cleanse the body. If you do not pray, you behave inadvisedly and most unwisely, supporting, gratifying and strengthening your body in every way, but neglecting your soul.

The best moments on earth are those in which we meditate upon heavenly things, or when we recognise and defend the truth, which is of, and from, the heavens. Only then do we truly live. It is therefore vital to the soul that we should more often rise above the earth, and mount to heaven, where alone is our true life, our true country which shall have no end.

The Lord our Heavenly Father knows, even before we ask, what things we have need of, what we want; but we do not know him as we ought, for we give ourselves up to worldly vanity, instead of committing ourselves into his hands. Therefore, in his wisdom and mercy he turns our needs into a pretext for us to turn to him.

Our prayers are necessary precisely to strengthen our faith, through which alone we can be saved: *By grace are ye saved through faith*. And: *O woman, great is thy faith*. For this reason the Lord made the woman pray earnestly, in order to awaken her faith and strengthen it.

God desires that we should frequently turn to him in prayer, in order to draw to himself his children, who have become hardened by sin and have withdrawn themselves from him, in order to cleanse us and enfold us in his love, in order to show us that he always has some blessing for us. Thus do good parents act towards evil-natured children.

Why is lengthy prayer necessary? In order that by prolonged fervent prayer we may warm our cold hearts, hardened in prolonged vanity. For it is strange to suppose that the heart, hardened in worldly vanity, can speedily be penetrated during prayer by the warmth of faith and the love of God, and stranger still to demand this of it. No—labour, great and repeated effort, is needed to attain this end. *The kingdom of heaven suffereth violence, and the violent take it by force*. The kingdom of heaven does not soon come into the heart, when men themselves flee from it so assiduously. The Lord himself makes clear his will that our prayers should not be short, by giving us for an example the importunate widow who often came to the judge, and troubled him with her requests.

Our soul cannot remain idle: it does good or evil, one of the two—wheat grows in it, or tares. But as every good comes from God, and as the means of getting every good from God is prayer, those who pray fervently, sincerely, from the depths of their hearts, obtain from the Lord grace to do good, and, before all, the grace of faith; whilst those who do not pray naturally remain without these spiritual gifts, depriving themselves of them, of their own will, by their own negligence and spiritual coldness; and as the wheat of good thoughts, inclinations, intentions, and works, grows in the hearts of those who labour in fervent prayer to the Lord, so in the hearts of those who do not pray the tares of every evil grow, smothering the small amount of good that has remained in them from the grace of baptism, chrism, and subsequent penitence and communion.

We must by every means implant in the field of our heart the seeds of the virtues: faith, hope in God, love for God and our neighbour. We must fertilise it by prayer, patience and good works; and not for a single hour must we be completely idle and inactive, for in times of idleness and inactivity the enemy zealously sows his tares. *While men slept, his enemy came, and sowed tares among the wheat, and went his way.*

We must carefully tend the field of our heart, lest the tares of every vice should grow in it; we must daily weed it—at least by morning and evening prayers—and water it with abundant tears, as with rain.

Our heart dies spiritually every day. Only ardent, tearful prayer can restore it to breath and life. If we do not pray fervently every day we may easily and speedily be overtaken by spiritual death.

The only means by which you can spend the day in perfect holiness, and peace, and without sin, is most sincere prayer as soon as you rise from sleep in the morning. It will bring Christ into your heart, with the Father and the Holy Ghost, and will thus strengthen your soul against any evil; but it will still be necessary for you carefully to guard your heart.

Never sleep before saying evening prayers, lest your heart become gross from ill-timed sleep, and lest the enemy should hinder it by a stony insensibility during prayer. *Be sober, be vigilant. Watch and pray, that ye enter not into temptation. Watch therefore, for ye know neither the day nor the hour wherein the Son of Man cometh. Watch ye therefore; for ye know not when the master of the house cometh—at even, or at midnight, or at cock-crow, or in the morning; lest coming suddenly he find you sleeping. And what I say unto you I say unto all—Watch.*

TWO

Thanksgiving

With sincere Christians prayer is continual, because we continually sin; gratitude is perpetual, because every day, every moment, we receive fresh mercies from God, beside the old mercies, which are numberless. Praise is also perpetual, because we perpetually see the glory of God's works in ourselves and in the world, especially the glory of his infinite love towards us.

You have fallen of your own free-will, corrupted by sin: this ought to be your most powerful incentive to prayer. Daily you receive great mercy from God: this ought to be a powerful incentive to thank God. Daily you contemplate the works of God's omnipotence, wisdom and goodness: this also ought to be an incentive to daily praise.

How infinitely God loves men, and cares for them, having not spared even his only-begotten Son, whom he gave to save us, and to bring us to the heavenly kingdom. It is impossible not to praise God when you remember that you were created from nothing, that from the beginning of time you were predestined to eternal blessedness, entirely without cause, due to no merits of your own—when you remember what grace God has bestowed upon you throughout your life, that you may be saved, and what a countless multitude of sins are forgiven you, and this not once or twice, but time after time after time.

Thank God every day with your whole heart for having given to you life according to his image and likeness—an intelligently free and immortal life. Especially thank him for having restored you unto life eternal after you had fallen into eternal death, and for having so done not simply by his omnipotence, for this would not have been in conformity with his justice, but by giving his only-begotten Son to redeem us, who suffered for us even unto death. Thank him also for bestowing new life upon you every day, upon you who have fallen countless times, of your own free-will, into sins, from life unto death, and for doing so as soon as you only say from your heart: *Father, I have sinned against heaven and before thee!*

Thank God also for often delivering you from sickness, you who imprudently throw yourself into danger and illness, the precursors of bodily death; for correcting your faults, and for not depriving you of earthly life, knowing that it is dear to you, and that you are not yet ready for the future life, life eternal. Thank him for all the means of existence, for all the joys and sorrows of life: for everything is from him, the all-merciful Father, the first origin of life, who has lent life to all.

Why should we thank God, and charitable persons, for everything? Primarily for our own benefit, to refine the feelings of our soul; to cultivate the feeling of dependence in all things upon God and good men, and grateful love towards them, as well as the feeling of our own nothingness without God, and our inability to live without the help of kind people.

THREE

Intercession

Pray for others as you would pray for yourself, for we are one, as the children of the Heavenly Father.

When you pray, endeavour to pray more for others than for yourself alone, and during prayer represent vividly to yourself all men as forming one body with yourself, and each separately as a member of the Body of Christ and your own member, *for we are members one of another*. Pray for all as you would pray for yourself, with the same sincerity and fervour; look upon their infirmities and sicknesses as your own, their spiritual ignorance, their sins and lusts, as your own, their temptations, misfortunes and manifold afflictions as your own. Such prayer will be accepted with great favour by the Heavenly Father, the most gracious, common Father of all, whose boundless love embraces and preserves all creatures.

It is pleasing to the Lord, as to a most loving Father, when we pray for others—his children; and as parents, at the request of their good children, forgive their wicked ones, so also the Heavenly Father, at the prayer of those that are his, or at the prayer of his priests for the people, has mercy even upon the unworthy.

It pleases the Lord, the common Father of all, when we pray for each other willingly with faith and love, for he is love, ready to forgive all for the sake of the love they bear one to another. The Holy Ghost said, *Pray one for another, that ye may be healed.*

You desire some spiritual blessing, for yourself, or for some-one else, or for all, but the Lord desires the same long, long before you, and is ready to grant it to you and others: the one thing that is needful is readiness to accept the divine gift. It only requires some worthiness in those who are to receive it, for God is infinite mercy, infinite goodness, and is always ready to grant every blessing, and often bestows it even before we ask for it, and in every case *is able to do exceeding abundantly above all that we ask or think.* Therefore it is always with boldness that I ask spiritual blessings of the Lord, and temporal blessings also, when these are needful, and the Lord grants them, in accordance with his faithful promise: *Ask, and it shall be given you; seek, and ye shall find; knock, and it shall be opened unto you: for every one that asketh receiveth; and he that seeketh findeth; and to him that knocketh it shall be opened.*

He that spared not his only Son, how shall he not with him also freely give us all things? The essential, the greatest, gift is given; everything else that we ask or pray for is infinitely less than the Son of God. We may therefore ask God for everything, trustfully, in the name of Jesus Christ, every blessing or gift that we can think of, for *Whatsoever ye shall ask in my name, that will I do, that the Father may be glorified in the Son.* Do you pray for the forgiveness of the sins, or for the repose of the souls, of the departed? *He is the propitiation for the sins of the whole world. The Blood of Jesus Christ his Son cleanseth us from all sin.* He can forgive even the departed every sin committed by them in word, deed or thought. *He is the resurrection, the life and the repose of his departed servants.* Would you ask anything of him for the living, and for yourself? *Ask what ye will, and it shall be done unto you.*

The Lord has full respect for nature, which he has created, and for her laws, as the products of his own infinite and perfect wisdom: for this reason he usually accomplishes his will through nature and her laws—for instance when he punishes men or blesses them. Therefore do not require miracles of him without extreme necessity.

It is good for me to pray for men when I partake worthily, with awareness, of the Holy Communion: then the Father, and the Son and the Holy Ghost, my God, is within me, and I feel great boldness before him. Then the King is within me as in his abode: I may ask what I will. *We will come unto him, and make our abode with him. Ye shall ask what ye will, and it shall be done unto you.*

Do not lose any opportunity of praying for any man, either at his request, or at the request of his relatives, friends, of those who esteem him, or of his acquaintances. The Lord looks favourably upon the prayer of our love, and upon our boldness before him.

When you are asked to pray that someone may be saved from bodily death, for instance, from drowning, from death through any sickness, from fire, or from any other disaster, commend the faith of those who ask you to do so, and say in yourself: 'Blessed be your faith; according to your faith may the Lord fulfil my unworthy feeble prayer, and may he increase my faith.'

Prayer for others is very beneficial to the man himself who prays; it purifies the heart, strengthens faith and hope in God, and arouses love for God and our neighbour.

When you are struck by other people's suffering, and the torment of their souls, so that you are induced to pray for them with a pitying and contrite heart, pray to God to have mercy upon them, and to forgive them their sins, as you would pray for the forgiveness of your own sins—that is, implore God with tears to pardon them; likewise pray for the salvation of others as you would pray for your own salvation.

If you make a habit of praying for the salvation of others, God will give you an abundance of spiritual gifts, the gifts of the Holy Spirit, who loves the soul that cares for the salvation of others, because he himself wishes to save us all by every possible means, if only we do not oppose him, and do not harden our hearts. *The Spirit itself maketh intercession for us with groanings which cannot be uttered.*

Why has our sincere prayer for others such great power over them? Because by cleaving to God during prayer I become one spirit with him, and unite with myself, by faith and love, those for whom I pray; for the Holy Spirit acting in me acts also at the same time in them, for he accomplishes all things. *We being many are one bread, and one body. There is one Body, and one Spirit.*

When you pray for others—for instance, for the members of your household, or for strangers, even though they may not have asked you to do so—pray for them with the same ardour and zeal as you would pray for yourself. Remember the commandment: *Thou shalt love they neighbour as thyself.*

Be not slothful in praying fervently for others—when asked, or of your own accord—and together with them; you will get a recompense from God—the grace of God in your heart, which shall gladden you, and strengthen you in faith and love for God and your neighbour. These words are true: they are taken from experience. In general we do not pray very willingly for others, but rather from duty and habit, and without our heart fully participating in the prayer: we must force ourselves to pray from the whole heart, with great faith, with great boldness, that we may obtain great and rich mercy from the bountiful God.

When you say a prayer for all men, but do not pray from your heart for all men, then your soul is oppressed, for God does not favour such prayer; but as soon as you begin to pray from your heart, at once you are no longer oppressed, for the Lord listens mercifully to such prayers.

When we pray for others, the words of our prayer must not be merely run over with the tongue, as if we were turning over the leaves of a book, or counting money: the water must flow as a stream of *living* water from its source—the words must come from the heart, they must not be a strange borrowed garment.

When we pray for the living and the departed by name, we must pronounce these names lovingly, and from a whole heart as though we bore in our souls the persons whom we name, remembering that they are our members, and members of the Lord's body. It is not right to stand before God and merely run over the names with the tongue.

We must remember that God sees into the heart, and that brotherly love and sympathy for those for whom we pray is a Christian duty. . . . There is a great difference between repeating names apathetically and remembering them heartily: the one is as far from the other as heaven is from earth.

We must pray fervently for all those enslaved by vices, for the enemy works within them.

When you see faults and vices in your neighbour, pray for him; pray for everybody, even for your enemy.

If you wish to correct the faults of anyone, do not think of trying to do so solely by your own means: you would only do harm by your own vices, for instance by pride and the irritability arising from it; *but cast thy burden upon the Lord*, and pray with all your heart that God himself will enlighten the mind and heart of that man. If he sees that your prayer breathes love, and that it really comes from the depths of your heart, he will undoubtedly fulfil it, and you will soon see, from the change that has taken place in him for whom you prayed, that it is the work of the most high God.

You do not want to pray for the man whom you hate and despise; but you must do so, and have recourse to the great physician, for you yourself are spiritually sick, with malice and pride. Your enemy, or the one whom you despise, is also sick; pray that the gentle Lord may teach you gentleness and patience, that he may teach and strengthen you to love your enemies, and not only those who wish you well, that he may teach you to pray for the evil-disposed as well as for the well-disposed.

We must not return anger for anger, pride for pride; those who are angry or proud towards us we must pity as overcome by the flames of hell, and by spiritual death; we must pray for them from the depths of our hearts, that the Lord may take away the darkness from them, enlighten them by the light of his grace.

The dead live. *God is not a God of the dead, but of the living; for all live unto him.* The soul hovers invisibly round the body, and the places where it liked to dwell. If it died in sin, then it cannot help to free itself from its bonds, and is in great need of the prayers of the living, especially those of the Church, the most holy Bride of Christ. Let us therefore pray earnestly for the dead. It is of great benefit to them—of more benefit than to the living.

Some ask, What is the use of naming the departed, or of praying for them? God himself knows the names and needs of all. But those who so speak forget, or do not know, the importance of prayer, do not realise the importance of every word uttered from a whole heart; they forget that the justice and mercy of God are moved by our heartfelt prayer, which the Lord in his goodness imputes to the merit of the living or the departed themselves, as to the members of the one body of the Church. They do not know that the *Church of the first-born, whose names are written in heaven,* in her love continually prays to God for us, and expressly names before God those who pray for them—equal for equal. We name them, and they name us. But he who does not lovingly remember his brethren in prayer will not himself be remembered, and does not deserve to be named. Even one word of faith and love means much in prayer: *The effectual fervent prayer of a righteous man availeth much.*

When you pray for the repose of the departed, force yourself to pray with your whole heart, remembering that to do so is a vital duty.

Represent to yourself how necessary repose is to the departed one, and how greatly he or she needs the prayers of the living, as a member of the one body of the Church; how the demons contest with the angels for his or her soul, and how it trembles, not knowing what its eternal destiny will be. Our prayer of faith and love for the departed means much in our Lord's sight. Represent also to yourself how necessary rest is for you, when you are bound by the fetters of sin, and how fervently and sincerely you then pray to the Lord and his immaculate Mother, and how glad you are when your fervent prayer brings you forgiveness of sins and peace of heart. Apply all this to the soul of the departed, which needs prayer—your prayer—now because it can no longer pray effectively itself; it needs also the rest which you can implore for it by ardent prayer and works of charity offered for the benefit of that soul, and above all by the offering of the unbloody sacrifice on its behalf.

Pray for the departed as though your own soul were in hell, in the flame; as though you yourself were in torment. Feel the torment of the departed with your whole heart, and pray most ardently that they may rest in peace, in the place of light and green pastures, in the place of refreshment.

Pray to the Lord for the repose of the souls of your departed forebears and brethren each day, at morning and at evening, in order that the remembrance of death may live in you, and that hope in the life to come, after death, may not become extinct in you; and that your spirit may daily be humbled by the thought of the transitory nature of your life.

FOUR

The fruits of prayer

Through the prayer of faith we can obtain from the all-merciful God all spiritual blessings, and all indispensable earthly blessings as well, if only our prayer is fervent, and our longing for these blessings sincere.

There is great benefit from prayer to those who pray: it gives rest to the soul and to the body—and rest not only to the soul of him who prays, but to the souls of our departed forebears and brethren also.

Prayer refreshes and enlivens the soul, as outer air refreshes the body. When we pray we feel stronger and fresher, as we feel physically and spiritually stronger and fresher when we walk in the fresh air.

A lively sense of God's presence is a source of peace and joy to the soul, whereas doubt in his presence produces distress, affliction and oppression. Heartfelt prayer is the source of peace at heart, whereas prayer that is superficial, insincere, in-attentive, injures the heart.

The sign of the Lord's mercy, or that of his immaculate Mother, to us, after or during prayer, is peace of heart—especially after we have been overcome by some vice, whose property is the absence of spiritual peace. By this peace of heart, and a kind of holy tenderness, we can also easily recognise that our prayer has been heard, and that the grace asked in it has been granted to us. The success of the prayer may also be recognised by the spiritual power, which we inwardly obtain for the fulfilment of the works of our calling, and by the inner light, which manifestly enters into our soul.

The Lord does not forsake those who labour for him, and who stand long before him; for with what measure they mete, he will measure to them in return, and he will reward them for the abundance of the sincere words of their prayer by sending into their souls a corresponding abundance of spiritual light, warmth, peace and joy.

It is good for me to draw near to God, said David, who had tasted the sweetness of prayer, and of the praise of God. Other men confirm this, and I, a sinner, also. Observe, that to draw near to God is a good and blessed thing, even here on earth, while we are yet in the sinful flesh. What bliss, then, will it be to be united to God there in heaven! And the bliss of union with God here on earth is a specimen and a pledge of the bliss of union with God after death, in eternity.

III

THE MANNER OF PRAYER

ONE

The Spirit of Prayer

Prayer is a golden link connecting the Christian man, the wanderer and stranger upon earth, with the spiritual world of which he is a member, and above all, with God, the source of life. The soul came forth from God, and to God may it ever ascend through prayer.

Prayer is the lifting up of the mind and heart to God, the contemplation of God, the daring converse of the creature with the Creator, the soul standing reverently before him, as before the King, before Life himself, who gives life to all.

Prayer is the constant feeling of our own spiritual poverty and infirmity, the contemplation in ourselves, in others, and in nature, of the works of the great wisdom and mercy, and almighty power, of God; it is a continually grateful frame of mind.

The foundation of prayer is the yearning of the image towards its prototype, as of like to like.

God is truth, and my prayer should be truth as well as life; God is light, and my prayer should be offered in the light of the mind and the heart; God is fire, and my prayer should be ardent; God is perfectly free, and my prayer should be the free outpouring of the heart.

Prayer is the living water, by means of which the soul quenches its thirst. When you pray, represent to yourself God alone before you, God in Trinity, and none other beside him. Represent to yourself that God is in the world as the soul is in the body, though he is infinitely greater than the world, and is not limited by it. Your body is small, and it is wholly penetrated by your finite soul; the world is large, but God is infinitely great, and fills the whole creation—*Who is everywhere present, and filleth all things.*

Remember that when standing in prayer you stand before God himself, who is all wisdom. Therefore, your prayer should be, so to say, all spirit, all understanding.

Think well before whom you stand, with whom you converse, to whom you sing; be wholly in God, belong to him alone, pray with all your heart, sing with all your heart, serve for your neighbour as for yourself, gladly, wholeheartedly, not with a divided heart and mind.

As an ill-natured man, coming with a request to one who is kind, gentle and meek, for the greater success of his request tries to resemble him, so the Christian, approaching God, or His immaculate Mother, or the angels and saints, in prayer, ought to try to resemble as far as possible the Lord himself, or his immaculate Mother, or the angels and saints. In this lies the secret of drawing near to God, and of his hearing our prayers speedily.

All you who draw near to serve God in prayer, learn to be like him—meek, humble and pure of heart; do not let there be any deceit or duplicity or coldness in your soul. Strive to have his Spirit, for *if any man have not the Spirit of Christ, he is none of his.* The Lord seeks in us that which is like to himself, onto which his grace may be grafted.

If you have not the time to say all the prayers, it does not matter, and you will receive incomparably greater benefit from praying fervently and not hurriedly than if you had said all your prayers hurriedly and without feeling.

It is well to pray long and continually, but *all men cannot receive this saying, save they to whom it is given.* It is better for those who are not capable of long prayers to say short prayers, but with a fervent spirit.

Prayer may become either a house built on sand, or a house built on a rock. Those build on sand who pray without faith, absently, coldly; such prayer is scattered of itself, and brings no profit to him who prays. Those build on a rock who, during the whole time of their prayer, have their eyes fixed upon God, and pray to him as to a living person, conversing face to face.

During prayer, it is necessary, in the first place, that the object of the prayer should be definitely expressed, or at least, that there should be a clear sense of it and desire for it in the heart; in the second place, it is necessary that this desire should be expressed with feeling and lively trust in the mercy of the Lord; in the third place, there must be a firm resolve not to sin in future, and to fulfil God's will in all things.

When a man is about to pray, he must humble his proud heart, must cast away from it earthly vanity, and must bring into it living and undoubting faith.

Always remember, when you pray, that the Lord will give you according to your heart. If you pray with faith, sincerely, with all your heart, not hypocritically, the Lord will reward you accordingly. And on the other hand, the colder your heart, the more doubting and hypocritical, the more useless will be your prayer—and more: so much the more will it anger the Lord, who seeks to be worshipped in spirit and in truth.

TWO

Faith in Prayer

Prayer is founded upon faith. As in this life we are guided in many things by faith and hope, so much more in relation to the spiritual world should we *walk by faith, not by sight.*

During prayer it is necessary to have such faith, that there should not for a single moment be any secret doubt, or any secret thought in the heart, that God does not hear us; it is also necessary that the soul should represent God before itself during the whole time of its converse with him, as with a king.

When you pray, whether inwardly only, or both inwardly and outwardly, be firmly convinced that the Lord is there, beside you and within you, and hears every word, even if it is uttered only within yourself, even when you only pray mentally; speak from your whole heart, sincerely, and likewise judge yourself sincerely, without in the least justifying

30

yourself; have faith that the Lord will have mercy upon you —and you will not remain unforgiven.

In order that, during prayer, you should have steadfast assurance of receiving every spiritual blessing from the Lord, believe that by uniting yourself unto the Lord during your prayer you become one spirit with him, and that God is most gracious, almighty, and most wise.

The chief thing in prayer, for which we must care above all, is lively clear-sighted faith in the Lord. Represent him vividly before you and in you: then ask of Jesus Christ in the Holy Spirit whatever you desire, and you will obtain it. Ask simply, without the slightest doubt: then God will be everything to you, accomplishing in an instant great and wonderful things. Ask both spiritual and material blessings, not only for yourself, but for all believers, for the whole body of the Church, not separating yourself from other believers, but spiritually uniting yourself with them, as a member of the one great body of the Church of Christ, and loving all, as your brethren or children in Christ, as the case may be. The Heavenly Father will fill you with great peace and boldness.

When we pray, we must believe in the power of the words of the prayer, in such a manner as not to separate the words from the deeds they express; we must believe that the deeds follow the words as the shadow follows the body, for the word and the deed of the Lord are indivisible: *He commanded, and they were created*. And likewise you must believe that that for which you ask in prayer will be done.

When you pray for anything, then consider the words, expressing your desire, your needs, as the very things, the very matter, for which you ask the Lord, and believe that you have already a sure pledge of receiving the objects of your prayer, in the very words by which these objects are designated, for the word itself may in an instant become deed with the Lord, and without fail you will receive that for which you ask, in return for your unshaken faith. *Ask, and it shall be given you.*

It is necessary that our hearts should burn during prayer with a desire for spiritual blessings, with love for God, and that we should vividly represent to ourselves his extreme mercy to mankind, and his readiness to hear all our prayers with fatherly love.

Remember that not a single word is lost during prayer, if you say it from the heart: God hears and weighs each word. Sometimes it seems to us that our words only strike the air in vain, and sound as the voice of one crying in the wilderness. No, no, it is not so. We must remember that God understands our words when we pray, just as those who pray perfectly themselves understand the words, for man is God's image. The Lord responds to every desire of the heart, whether expressed in words or not.

During prayer always firmly believe and bear in mind that all your thoughts and words can undoubtedly become deeds. *For with God nothing shall be impossible.* Even your words shall not be without power. *All things are possible to him that believeth.* Take heed of your words, for they are precious. *Every idle word that men shall speak, they shall give account of in the day of judgment.*

Remember that if you do not speak idly during prayer, but say the words of the prayer with feeling, then your words shall not return to you empty, but shall without fail bring you those fruits which are contained in them, as the fruit is enclosed in the shell.

Concerning the fulfilment of that which you ask in prayer: believe that it is incomparably easier for the Lord to fulfil your words than it is for you to pronounce them, and that if there is the word, there is also the deed; for with the Lord there is no word without the deed, and no word shall return unto him empty, according to his word. Remember constantly during prayer that God is He Who Is, and that from him everything proceeds; including both the thought of anything and the word of anything.

When you pray to the Lord believe that it is as easy and simple for the Lord to give any blessing to his people as for you to think of it. Besides, as God is ever-flowing, infinite goodness, he desires, and ever seeks, to impart his goodness to his creatures, if only they turn to Him in faith, hope and love, as children to their father, recognising their sinfulness, their poverty, need, blindness and infirmity without him.

When you doubt the possibility of the fulfilment of any of your prayers, remember that to God it is possible to give you all things excepting direct evil—that your word itself, your prayer itself, is already a sure guarantee that its fulfilment is possible: for if you can think of something possible or impossible to yourself, then this 'something' is absolutely possible to the Lord, to whom the thought is already deed, if he pleases to fulfil it. *Ask, and it shall be given you; seek, and ye shall find; knock, and it shall be opened unto you.* Add to this God's great wisdom, by which, in bestowing gifts upon us, he chooses that which is best for us, and which corresponds to our spiritual and bodily state. On your part all that is needed is firm, undoubting assurance in the possibility of the

Lord's fulfilment of your request, and also that your prayer should absolutely be good, for good, and not for anything evil.

God has granted us existence—the greatest gift of his goodness, and after we had fallen away from life unto death he gave us his Son to bring us back to life. How small by comparison are all the other gifts we ask of him in prayer, and how easy it is for him to give them to us at the first word of true faith, if they are really necessary to us. It is unpardonable in us if we still doubt that we shall get what we ask of God in prayer. The Lord said clearly: *Ask, and it shall be given you.*

He who prays should bear in mind that if God spared not even his only-begotten Son, but gave him for us all, he cannot but give us every imaginable blessing. For if the infinite and greatest blessing has been given, then will not the finite and lesser blessings also be granted? Our Heavenly Father gives us every blessing in Christ: *His divine power hath given unto us all things needful unto life and godliness, through the knowledge of him.*

Great encouragement and hope are afforded those who pray by the reassuring words of the Lord: *Ask, and it shall be given you,* and, further, *What man is there of you, whom if his son ask bread, will he give him a stone?* If anyone asks me anything, and I, evil and corrupt as I am, listen to his requests, his words moving my heart to pity and my hand to giving, then will not my words, my sincere prayer, move the Fount of mercy, the Lover of mankind, to have mercy upon me, and help me, a sinner, but still his creature and the work of his hands? If earthly fathers are merciful, will not the Heavenly Father be more so? *If ye then, being evil, know how to give good gifts unto your children, how much more shall your*

34

Father which is in heaven give good things to them that ask him?

If you have not a firm and unashamed faith in the most merciful and almighty God, do not hasten to pray to him to grant you any blessing, for if you do the Devil will strike and wound you with unbelief in the possibility of the fulfilment of your prayer, and you will depart from before the face of God gloomy, despondent and ashamed. Before you pray, reckon the degree of your faith, and having found it sufficient, lively, firm and unashamed, *come boldly unto the throne of grace, that you may obtain mercy and find grace to help in time of need.*

Our hope of obtaining that for which we ask during prayer is founded upon faith in God's abundant mercy, for he is the God of abundant mercy, and the Lover of men; therefore, when we pray, it is useful to remind ourselves of the innumerable experiences of mercy and grace bestowed upon men in Holy Writ and in the lives of the saints and also upon ourselves.

In order that prayer may be effectual, it is also necessary that those who pray should already have obtained that for which they have formerly asked, and firmly believe this with their whole heart. We often receive through prayer that for which we ask, especially when we pray for that which relates to the salvation of our soul; it is necessary to ascribe this directly to God and his grace, and not to chance.

During prayer, it is necessary always to have full hope of getting that for which we ask—for instance, deliverance from troubles, spiritual sickness, sins; for we have already a thousand times received mercy from the Lord, and well we know it, and therefore to doubt of our prayers being heard would be the greatest folly and blindness.

Many do not pray because it seems to them that God has not granted that for which they have prayed in the past, or because they consider it unnecessary to pray; they say that God knows everything without our asking, and forget that it is said: *Ask, and it shall be given you; seek, and ye shall find; knock, and it shall be opened unto you.* Such men do not see that they have no faith—the Christian's most precious inheritance, which is as necessary as life itself—and that they are going to destruction.

Is it not enough for you to see weakness in men? Do you wish to see weakness in God himself, secretly thinking that God cannot fulfil your prayer? To men many things are difficult, and many impossible; but how can you consider anything as difficult to God? Can anything be difficult or impossible to him? To him all things are possible, and nothing is difficult. When you pray, then, be firmly convinced that the Lord can do everything you ask in a moment. Do not ascribe your own inability to God! Remember that to him nothing is impossible, and ask boldly for everything, hoping to receive everything: *And all things, whatsoever ye shall ask in prayer, believing, ye shall receive.*

If you wish to ask of God any blessing, then prepare yourself before praying by undoubting and firm faith, and take precautions against doubt and unbelief in good time. For if during the prayer itself your heart wavers in its faith and does not stand firm, it will go ill with you: do not expect to obtain of the Lord that for which you have prayed doubtingly, for in so doing you have offended the Lord, and God does not bestow his gifts upon a reviler. *And all things, whatsoever ye*

shall ask in prayer, believing, ye shall receive, said the Lord.
This clearly implies that if you doubt and do not believe, you
will not receive. And again, *If ye have faith, and doubt not, ye
shall have power to move mountains.* Therefore, if you doubt
and do not believe, you shall not have power to do so.

Prayer breathes hope, and a prayer without hope is a sinful
prayer.

THREE

Wholeheartedness in Prayer

If you wish your prayer to give life, first of all strengthen
your heart in the Lord.

It is necessary to rouse the heart to pray, otherwise it will
become dry. The attributes of prayer must be, love of God,
sincerity and simplicity.

When we pray, we must absolutely subject the heart to the
will, and turn it towards God. It must not be cold, crafty,
untruthful, double-minded; if it is, what will be the use of
our prayers? It is good for us to hear God's anger: *This people
draweth nigh unto me with its mouth, and honoureth me with
its lips, but its heart is far from me.* So let us not stand in
church in a state of spiritual collapse, but let the spirit of each
at such a time burn in its working towards God.

If you have a rule to read so many prayers, whether they be long or short, fulfil your rule well; read them attentively, and do not do God's work with a divided heart, of which only one half belongs to him, and the other half to your own flesh.

Even men do not much value the services we render to them coldly, out of habit. And God requires our hearts: *My son, give me thine heart.* For the heart is the principal part of the man—his life. Indeed, the heart is the man himself. Thus he who does not pray with his heart does not pray at all, because only his body prays, and the body without the mind is nothing more than dust.

Let us measure the worth of our prayers by human measure, by the quality of our approach to other men. How do we behave to them? Sometimes we express ourselves to them coldly and heartlessly, out of duty or simply out of politeness, and it is the same when we do anything for them; whilst at other times we do so wholeheartedly, with warmth and love, often only pretended, but often really sincere. We are similarly inconstant with God. But this should not be. We must always glorify God, give thanks to him, and pray to him, with our whole heart. For it is with the whole heart that every work must be done in his sight, with the whole heart that he must be loved and trusted.

It is necessary to overcome oneself, to strive to pray with the whole heart, for it is a good and joyful thing to pray with the whole heart.

FOUR

Sincerity in Prayer

Sometimes during a lengthy prayer only a few minutes are really pleasing to God, and constitute true prayer, true service to him. The chief thing in prayer is the nearness of the heart to God.

Sometimes people call prayer that which is not prayer at all: for instance, a man goes to church, stands there for a time, looks at the icons or at other people, and says that he has prayed to God; or else he stands before an icon at home, bows his head, says some words he has learned by heart, without understanding, and without feeling, and says that he has prayed—although with his thoughts and his heart he has not prayed at all, but was elsewhere, with other people and other things, and not with God.

Did the Pharisees think that they prayed hypocritically? They did not think so; they considered themselves to be right in their hypocrisy itself. It had become their habit; it had become second nature to them; and they thought they were serving God by their prayer. Do the Christian hypocrites of the present day think that they pray and live hypocritically? They do not think so. They pray daily, perhaps at length; but they pray out of habit with their lips, not with their hearts; without heartfelt contrition, without a firm desire for amendment, and only in order to fulfil the established rule, and *think* they do

God service, whilst in fact they only incur the wrath of God. We all sin, more or less, in praying hypocritically, and we shall be greatly censured for it.

Many people pray hypocritically, and hypocritical prayer becomes a habit with them; they do not themselves observe, and do not wish to observe, that they pray hypocritically, and not in spirit and in truth, so that if anybody were to accuse them of praying hypocritically they would be angry at such an absurdity, as they would hold it to be.

Men become hypocritical not suddenly but gradually. At first, perhaps, they pray whole-heartedly, but afterwards—for to pray with the whole heart is always difficult; we always have to force ourselves to it—they begin to pray superficially, with their lips, not from the depths of the soul, for this is easier. Finally, at the increased assaults of the Devil, they pray *only* with their lips, the prayer not reaching the heart at all.

Our heart often sleeps during prayer: the outer man prays, but not the inner one. Often during prayer we only flatter with our tongue.

How often it happens in life that a man has one thing in his heart and another on his lips, and wears two faces at one and the same time. It is the same during prayer, before God himself, who knows the secrets of the heart; in prayer also a man frequently wears two faces, saying one thing and having another in his heart and thoughts. If, which happens still more frequently, a man does not sympathise in his heart with what he is saying, although he understands and thinks about it, then he is throwing the words to the air, and he deceives himself if he believes that he can please God by such a prayer. This is strange and sinful duplicity. It is a bitter fruit and evidence of our fall into sin.

Outward prayer is often performed at the expense of inward prayer, and inward at the expense of outward. That is to say, if, when I pray with my lips, or read prayers, many of the words do not penetrate the heart, I become double-minded and hypocritical; with my lips I say one thing, and in my heart I feel another. The lips speak the truth, but the heart does not agree with the words of the prayer. But if I pray inwardly and whole-heartedly, then, I concentrate upon the contents and power of the words, rather than upon pronouncing them, in this way gradually accustoming my heart to the truth, and entering into the spirit of the prayer. In this way I accustom myself, little by little, to pray in spirit and truth, in accordance with the words of him who is Eternal Truth: *They that worship him must worship him in spirit and in truth*.

Every insincere prayer removes your heart from God, and sets it in enmity to you yourself, whilst every earnest prayer draws your heart nearer to God, and helps to make it enduringly godly.

During prayer do not allow the enemy, acting through the flesh, to conquer you; speak the truth from your heart, and let your tongue utter no falsehood. Think and feel what you say in prayer, and do not let there be honey on your tongue and ice in your heart.

How can we teach ourselves to speak the truth from our heart during prayer? We must bring every word of the prayer down to our heart, lay it to heart, feel its truth in our heart, be convinced of our need of that for which we ask, or of the need of heartfelt gratitude for God's great and innumerable benefits to us.

It seems habitual to our heart to lie, both in prayer, and in our intercourse with other men. The heart is a pillar of falsehood.

The Christian must make use of every means to eradicate all falsehood from his heart, and to implant in it pure truth. We must begin with prayer, as with a matter in which truth is indispensable before all else, in accordance with the Lord's own words: *Worship him in spirit and in truth. Speak the truth from your heart.* When we have learnt to speak the truth from our heart during prayer, we shall not allow ourselves to lie in everyday life: sincere, true prayer, having cleansed our heart from falsehood, will also protect it from falsehood in our relations with others.

It is sometimes necessary to ask a person who prays for himself or for others, this question, in order to rouse his slumbering heart and conscience: Are you really in need of that for which you are apparently asking; do you really desire to obtain it? Do you sincerely desire—for instance—amendment and holiness of life for yourself and others?

He who prays must hunger after those blessings—above all, the spiritual ones: the forgiveness of sins, the hallowing, the strengthening in virtue—for which he prays; otherwise it will be a useless waste of words.

Some seem to be praying to the Lord, but are really serving the Devil, who nestles in their hearts, because they pray only with their lips, whilst their hearts are cold, and neither feel nor desire that which the lips ask, and are far from the Lord.

The name of the Lord himself, that of his immaculate Mother, and those of the holy angels and saints, must always be pronounced from a pure heart, with burning faith and love.

It is sometimes well during prayer to say a few words of our own, breathing fervent faith, and love for God. Let us not always converse with him in the words of others, let us not for ever remain children in faith and hope; we must show also our own mind, we must *indite a good matter* from our own heart also. Moreover, we grow too accustomed to the words of others, and consequently grow cold in prayer. And how pleasing to the Lord is this lisping of our own, coming directly from a believing, loving and thankful heart.

When you truly pray to God in your own words the soul trembles with joy, with fire, with life, with bliss. You will utter few words, but you will know blessedness such as you would not have found from saying the longest and most moving prayers of others, pronounced out of habit, and insincerely.

Forced prayer develops hypocrisy, and renders a man incapable of thoughtful, concentrated activity, and slothful in everything. This should persuade all who pray in this manner to correct themselves. We must pray gladly and energetically, from the whole heart. Likewise, do not pray to God only when you are obliged to, in sorrow or in need, for *God loveth a cheerful giver*.

FIVE

Humility in Prayer

During prayer, intentional, deliberate, extreme humility is indispensable; humility destroys all the snares of the enemy. But how much secret pride, how much sophistry, there is in us!

This, we say, I know; this is not for me; this is superfluous; in that I am not a sinner.

The insensibility of the heart during prayer to the truth of the words uttered proceeds from the heart's unbelief, and from its insensibility to its own sinfulness; and these in turn emanate from a secret pride. In accordance with the measure of his feelings during prayer a man may recognise whether he is proud or humble; the more feeling, the more ardent, his prayer, the more humble he is; whilst the more unfeeling and cold it is, the prouder he is.

In the prayers of the Orthodox Church some sins are enumerated, but not all; and often the very sins by which we have bound ourselves are not named; it is therefore absolutely necessary that we enumerate them ourselves during our prayer, clearly recognising their gravity with humility and heartfelt contrition. This is why at the confession of sins in evening prayers provision is made for us to mention particular sins.

During prayer a sincere seeking after amendment is indispensable.

IV

THE DIFFICULTY OF PRAYER

Perseverance in Prayer

We soon grow weary of praying. Why? Because we do not vividly represent to ourselves the Lord, who is at our right hand. Look upon him unceasingly with the eyes of your heart, and then, even if you stand praying all night, you will not grow weary. What do I say—all night? You will be able to stand praying two and three nights without growing weary.

One who during prayer became lethargic, and feeble in mind and body, and longed to sleep, roused himself by saying, With whom art thou conversing, my soul? And after this, by representing the Lord vividly before him, he began to pray with great feeling and tears; his blunted attention was sharpened, his mind and heart were enlightened, and he himself wholly revived. This shows us what it is to represent the Lord vividly to ourselves, and to walk in his presence!

People say that if you do not feel inclined to pray it is better not to pray; but this is crafty carnal sophistry. If you pray only when you are inclined to, you will cease praying altogether; this is what the flesh desires. *The kingdom of heaven suffereth violence.* You will not be able to work out your salvation without forcing yourself.

It is necessary continually to force ourselves to truth and goodness; when praying, we must every moment force ourselves to pronounce each word with power, truly from the heart. When we do not force ourselves to sincerity, the prayer will be hypocritical, false and ungodly. We must say the words of the prayer in such a way that they persuade ourselves: if they are persuasive to us, they will also be persuasive to God; but without persuading yourself do not think to persuade God by your prayer to grant any blessing you ask for.

Learn to pray; force yourself to prayer. In the beginning it will be difficult; but afterwards the more you force yourself to pray, the more easily you will do so. But in the beginning it is always necessary to force oneself.

Do not indulge your slothful flesh during prayer. Do not hurry. The flesh, growing weary and oppressed by the holy work, hastens to finish praying, in order to rest, or to occupy itself with worldly or carnal matters.

Be assured, if you hurry over your prayers to give rest to your body, you will lose both spiritual and bodily rest. What labour, sweat and tears, are needed that our hearts may approach God.

Learn not to let your spirit sleep even for a moment during your prayer; pray in spirit and in truth, unremittingly, and not flattering the Lord by one word—that is, not pronouncing a single word insincerely or hypocritically. Let your prayer express only truth, let it be the utterance of the Holy Spirit, and let it not serve the lying enemy by a single word, nor be in any way the organ of the Devil. And to release your soul from his heavy load, and to quench his fire, pray fervently to God, heartily confessing your fault before him—your hypocrisy during prayer—and he will deliver you, and give you peace. Do not hurry; say and do everything calmly. You will succeed. It is the enemy who urges us to hurry, and disturbs us, for there is no sense in confused hurry.

Are you in a hurry to get to your place of service or work? Get up earlier; do not sleep so long; and pray fervently—you will get calm, energy and success for your whole day's work.

You want to finish your rule of prayer quickly, in order to rest your weary body? Pray fervently, and you will enjoy peaceful, calm and healthy sleep. Do not hurry, then; nor say your prayers anyhow—by half an hour's prayer you will gain three whole hours of the soundest sleep.

Do not spare yourself, but pray earnestly, even if you have been working hard all day. Do not be negligent in prayer; address God throughout your prayer from your whole heart, for it is a duty you owe to him. Having put your hand to the plough, do not look back. If you allow yourself to pray carelessly, and not from your heart, you will not fall asleep— if you are praying at night—until you have wiped out your sin by tears. This is not so with everybody, of course, but only with the more perfect. Take care, then, not to put your flesh before God, and for his sake spurn bodily repose.

TWO

The Ordering of Prayer

When praying in the evening, do not forget to confess to the Holy Spirit, in really sincere and contrite prayer, those sins into which you have fallen during the past day. A few moments of fervent repentance, and you will be cleansed by the Holy Spirit from every impurity; you will be whiter than snow, and tears, purifying the heart, will flow from your eyes; you will be covered with the garment of Christ's righteousness, and united to him, and to the Father and the Holy Spirit.

During the night the soul is free from worldly vanity, and therefore the spiritual world can act upon it, can impress itself upon it, more freely; so that, if a man is righteous, the thoughts and desires of his heart are the thoughts and desires of the Lord himself, or of the Angels and Saints; whilst if he is an unrepentant sinner, they are the thoughts and desires of the Devil himself.

The inner man, amidst worldly vanity, amidst the darkness of his flesh, is not so bound by the tempting devices of the evil one, and looks out more freely, early in the morning just after waking up, as a fish sometimes throws itself up playfully on the surface of the water. All the rest of the time he is enveloped in almost impenetratable darkness, his eyes are covered with a bandage, which conceals from him the true state of things spiritual and physical. Take advantage of these morning hours, which are the hours of a new life, of a life renewed by temporary sleep. They show us in part that state in which we shall be when we shall rise up renewed on that great and universal morning of the nightless day of resurrection, or when we shall rid ourselves of this mortal body.

Everything has its proper time. There may be an unfavourable time, even for prayer.

Be moderate in all devout works, for it is prudent and wise to be moderate, even in virtue, taking account of your energy, and the circumstances of time, place, and preceding labour.

It is well, for instance, to pray with a pure heart, but as soon as there is no correspondence between the prayer and your energy, in the circumstances of place and time, and your preceding labours, it ceases to be a virtue.

THREE

Hindrances to Prayer

When praying, a man must lay aside every worldly care, and care only for the salvation of his soul.

Is your heart impatient to go to vain, worldly matters? Master it; let its treasure be not earthly vanity, but God; teach it to attach itself through prayer to God, and not to worldly vanity, so that you may not be covered with shame in the day of sickness, and in the hour of death, like him who was rich in worldly vanity, but poor in faith, hope and love. If you do not pray as I say, you will prosper neither in life, nor in faith, nor in spiritual understanding.

Those who pray little are weak in heart, and thus, when they wish to pray, their hearts become enfeebled, and so do their hands, their bodies, their minds, and it is difficult for them to pray.

He who prays in a hurry, without whole-hearted understanding and feeling, being conquered by his slothful, sleepy flesh, serves not God, but his own flesh, his own self-love, and reviles God by his inattention and the indifference of his heart to prayer: *God is a spirit: and they that worship him must worship him in spirit and in truth*—not hypocritically. However slothful and weak your flesh may be, however inclined to sleep you may be, conquer yourself; do not spare yourself, for God; renounce yourself; let your gift to God be perfect; give God your heart.

Is it possible to pray rapidly without injuring the effect of the prayer? It is possible for those who have learned to pray inwardly with a pure heart. During prayer it is necessary that your heart should really desire that for which you ask, should feel the truth of what you are saying, and this comes naturally to a pure heart. That is why it is able to pray rapidly, and at the same time agreeably, as in this case the rapidity does not injure the sincerity of the prayer. But for those who have not yet learned to pray sincerely, it is necessary to pray slowly, pausing for each word of the prayer to arouse a corresponding echo. And this is not always soon given to men unaccustomed to prayerful contemplation. For such men, therefore, it must be an absolute rule to pronounce the words of the prayer slowly and with pauses.

Do not allow your heart to be cold, above all during prayer. Often prayer is on the lips, but in the heart there is something very different, so that by the lips the man seems near to God, whilst in his heart he is far from him. And during our prayers the evil one makes use of every means to chill our hearts, and to fill them with hypocrisy in a manner imperceptible to us. Pray and fortify yourself; fortify your heart.

When you pray, keep to the rule that it is better to say five words from the depth of your heart than ten thousand words with your tongue only. When you observe that your heart is cold and prays unwillingly, stop praying and warm your heart by representing vividly to yourself your own wickedness, your spiritual poverty, misery and blindness, or the great benefits which God bestows every moment upon you and all mankind, especially upon Christians; and then pray slowly and fervently.

When you are saying your prayers—and especially if you have a rule of prayer according to a book, do not hurry from one word to another without feeling its truth, without laying it to your heart; always strive to feel with your heart the truth of that which you say. Your heart will oppose this—sometimes by slothfulness and stony insensibility, sometimes by doubt and unbelief, sometimes by distraction and deviation of the mind to earthly objects and cares, sometimes by the remembrance of the offences of your neighbour, and by a feeling of revenge and hatred towards him, sometimes by the representation of worldly pleasures, or by the representation of pleasure derived from reading novels and worldly books in general. Do not spare yourself; conquer your heart, and offer it to God as an acceptable sacrifice: *My son, give me thine heart.* Your prayer will unite you to God and all heaven, and you will be filled with the Spirit and the fruits of the Spirit—righteousness, peace, joy, love, meekness, long-suffering, and wholehearted repentance.

The heart that has fondness for food and drink, that is greedy for these, and is weakened by them, has no trust in prayer; nor has the heart in which hatred and animosity are concealed, nor that which is bound by avarice, covetousness and envy, until it puts these things away and amends itself.

FOUR

Despondency in Prayer

When you are praying, watch over yourself, so that not only your outward man prays, but your inward man also. Though you be sinful beyond measure, still pray. Do not heed the Devil, who will craftily provoke you to despair, but overcome and conquer his wiles. Remember the abyss of the Redeemer's mercy and love to mankind. The Devil will represent the Lord's face to you as terrible and unmerciful, rejecting your prayer and repentance, but do you remember the Lord's own words: *Him that cometh to me, I will in no wise cast out;* and again: *Come unto me, all ye that labour, and are heavy laden*—with sins and offences, and the wiles and lying slanders of the Devil—*and I will give you rest.*

When during prayer your heart is overwhelmed with despondency and melancholy, be sure that these proceed from the Devil, endeavouring by every means to hinder you in your prayer. Be firm, take courage, and by the remembrance of God drive away this deadly feeling.

During prayer there sometimes occur moments of deadly darkness and spiritual anguish arising from unbelief in the heart (for unbelief *is* darkness). Do not let your heart fail you at such moments, but remember that if the divine light has been cut off from you, it always shines in all its splendour in God himself, in his church, in heaven and on earth, and in the material world, in which *his eternal power and Godhead* are visible. Do not think that truth has failed, because truth is God himself, and everything that exists has its foundation and reason in him. Only your own weak sinful and darkened heart can fail in the truth, for it cannot always bear the strength of the light of truth, is often not capable of embracing its purity, except it be cleansed from its sins, the first cause of spiritual darkness. The proof of this you may find in yourself. When the light of faith or God's truth dwells in your heart, only then is it calm, firm, strong, and lively; but when this is cut off, then your heart becomes uneasy, weak as a reed shaken by the wind, and lifeless. Do not pay any attention to this darkness of Satan. Drive it away from your heart by making the sign of the life-giving cross.

When you are praying alone, and your spirit is dejected, and you are wearied and oppressed by your loneliness, remember then, as always, that God the Holy Trinity looks upon you with eyes brighter than the sun; and so do all the angels, including your own guardian, and all the saints of God. Truly they do; for they are all one in God, and where God is there are they also. Where the sun is, thither also are all its rays. Try to understand what this means. Bear in mind with whom you are conversing. Men often forget with whom they are conversing during prayer, and who are the witnesses of their prayer.

You are praying, your prayer is successfully accomplished, and you have inward proof that the Lord hears it, and accepts it favourably; your thoughts are at peace, and you feel light of heart; yet at the end of your prayer, through some slight weakness of your heart and thoughts, a heavy burden falls on your heart, and you feel an extreme difficulty in praying, and even a strong dislike for it, instead of the former lightness and desire to pray. Do not despair; these are only the snares of the enemy, who loves to mock at us, particularly at the end of our employment in prayer, so that we may fall into despondency, and consider all our labours in that holy work lost.

V

THE HELP OF THE CHURCH IN HEAVEN

ONE

The Mother of God

Through the incarnation of the Word the all-holy Virgin has been given to us as an all-powerful intercessor, who protects us from sins, misfortunes and disasters, praying for us day and night, our queen whose power no enemy—visible or invisible—can withstand, truly our mother by grace in accordance with the words uttered by Christ on the cross to the beloved disciple: *Behold thy mother!* and to her: *Behold thy son!*

Imagine how resplendently adorned, what a pure and perfect palace of the Almighty must have been the most holy soul and the most pure body of the Mother of God, in whose womb God the Word—Godhead, soul and body—came to dwell! Imagine how eternal, infinite, unchangeable is her holiness! Imagine of what reverence she is worthy, how we should glorify her!

The Mother of God is one flesh and blood, and one spirit with the Redeemer, as his Mother. So infinitely great, by the grace of God, was her merit, that she became the Mother of God himself, giving him immaculate and sacred flesh, nourishing him with her milk, carrying him in her arms, clothing him, caring in every way for him during his infancy, kissing and caressing him time without number. Who can describe the greatness of the Virgin Mother of God?

Know and remember that your salvation is always near to the heart of our Lady the Mother of God; for it was for this that God the Word chose her out of all generations, and took flesh of her—to save the human race from sin, from the curse and from eternal death, eternal torment. As he desires that we should be saved, so does she. Turn to her in full faith, trust, and love.

How holy must be the Mother of God, with whom God the Word himself, the Light everlasting, was most truly united—*the true light, which lighteneth every man that cometh into the world—whom the Holy Ghost came upon, and whom the power of the Most High overshadowed!* How holy—all-holy—must be the Mother of the Lord, who became the temple of God not made with hands, and was entirely penetrated, in all her thoughts, feelings, words and deeds, by the Holy Ghost; from whose blood the Creator himself made flesh for himself!

Truly she is most holy, firm, steadfast, immovable, unchangeable through all eternity in her most exalted God-given holiness; for the all-perfect God, her Son, has made her also all-perfect, on account of her great humility, of her love of purity and of the source of purity—God, of her entire abandonment of the world and entire attachment to the heavenly kingdom, and above all because she gave herself to him to be his Mother, bore him in her womb, and afterwards in her immaculate arms, nourished him with her immaculate milk—him, who feeds all creatures!—cared for him, caressed him, suffered and sorrowed for him, shed tears for him, lived her whole life for him alone, and was wholly absorbed in his Spirit, one heart and one soul with him, one holiness with him! How exalted, how wondrous, is the unity in love and holiness of the immaculate Virgin Mary with her Divine Son, the Lord Jesus Christ!

He who has adorned the heavens with stars, could he not still more beautifully adorn his chosen heaven, the immaculate Virgin his Mother? He who has adorned the earth with many coloured and fragrant flowers, could he not adorn his earthly Mother with all the flowers of virtue, making her fragrant with all spiritual perfumes? She is the temple of the Godhead, adorned with every beauty, and more fragrant than all earthly perfumes. May God in his mercy, at the prayers of his immaculate Mother, adorn me, who am disfigured by sin; may he make me, the unclean, fragrant.

The Mother of God is the most beautifully adorned temple of the Holy Trinity. After God, she is the treasury of all blessings —of purity, of holiness, of all true wisdom—the source of spiritual power and constancy.

It was for our sake that the Lord was incarnate, suffered even unto the death of the cross, and rose from the dead. It was for our sake also that he adorned his Mother, the immaculate Virgin Mary, with all virtues, and endued her with every divine power, so that she, the most merciful, the most perfect, should be, after himself, everything to us. And therefore let us not waste God's grace with which our Lady is filled. Let us come with boldness and trust to the immaculate Virgin, ever-helpful, ever-protecting. If sins trouble us, let us pray to her, that she may cleanse us with the hyssop of her prayers from every impurity of flesh and spirit.

The Virgin Mary is the most merciful queen of all the sons and daughters of men, as the daughter of God the Father, who is love; the mother of God the Word, who is our love; the chosen bride of the Holy Spirit, who is love one in substance with the Father and the Word. How can we not have recourse to such a queen, how not expect all spiritual blessings from her?

If foes surround you, and you are in spiritual distress, call at once upon our most holy Lady. She is queen in order that she may reign, by her sovereign power, over the powers that oppose us, and may mightily succour us, for we are her inheritance.

When you are about to pray to our Lady, be firmly assured that you will not depart from her without mercy. It is meet and right so to think, so to have confidence in her. She is the all-merciful Mother of the all-merciful God, and her merciful gifts—incalculably great, innumerable—have been declared from all ages by the Church. To pray to her without such assurance would be foolish and insolent, for such doubt would offend her goodness, just as God's goodness is offended when people pray to him without hoping to get what they pray for.

When you feel yourself to be an ungodly, impure, wicked, blasphemous sinner, and therefore unworthy to draw near to our Lady and pray to her, then is the very time to pray fervently to her, just because you feel yourself such a sinner. Do not sink in the mire of sin, but come to our Lady, stand before her image in sure hope of her presence, show her your sinful sores without shame, and your loathing for them, and ask her to cleanse you from this spiritual leprosy—you will not be put to shame. The all-merciful one will not despise you, the immaculate and most speedy helper will cleanse you, as the Lord himself cleansed the ten lepers.

When you look upon the image of the Mother of God, with her Eternal Child, marvel how most truly the Godhead was united with human nature, glorify God's omnipotent goodness, and recognising your own dignity as man live worthily of your high calling in Christ—the calling of a child of God, an inheritor of eternal bliss.

Hail, full of grace, the Lord is with thee! So does holy Church address the all-holy Virgin Mother of God. But the Lord is also with every devout soul that believes in him; it is not only with her that he abides: *The Lord is with thee*—these words may be addressed to everyone who keeps the Lord's commandments.

TWO

The Saints of God

How the Creator and Provider of all has honoured and adorned our nature! The saints shine with his light, they are hallowed by his grace, having conquered sin and washed away every sinful impurity of body and spirit; they are glorious with his glory, they are incorruptible through his incorruptibility. Glory to God, who has so honoured, enlightened, and exalted our nature!

What does the daily invocation of the saints signify—of different ones each day, during the whole year, and during our whole life? It signifies that God's saints, as our brethren—but perfect—live, and are near us, ever ready to help us, by the grace of God. We live together with them, in the house of our Heavenly Father, only in different parts of it. We live in the earthly, they in the heavenly half; but we can converse with them, and they with us.

How closely the Church in heaven and the Church on earth are connected! What love the Church has! She unceasingly remembers the Church in Heaven, she calls upon its members in prayer, and gives glory to them for the great deeds wrought upon earth for God's sake. She unceasingly prays for the whole body of the Church on earth, and intercedes for the departed, in the hope of the resurrection unto life eternal, and of union with God and the saints. Let us enter into the spirit of this great love of our mother the Orthodox Church, let us be penetrated with it. Let us look upon all our brethren as our own members, as we are all members of the one body of the Church, and let us love them actively, as we love ourselves. Then shall we be living members of the Church in heaven, and she will be our active and speedy helper and intercessor.

We ought to have the most lively spiritual union with the dwellers in heaven, the apostles, prophets, martyrs, saintly bishops, confessors, with all the saints, as they are all members of the one body, the Church of Christ, to which we sinners also belong, and the living Head of which is the Lord Jesus Christ himself. This is why we call upon them in prayer, converse with them, thank and praise them. It is urgently necessary for every Christian to be in union with them if he desires to make Christian progress; for the saints are our friends, our guides to salvation, who pray and intercede for us.

As in the earthly life there are poor and rich, so also in the spiritual life, in the spiritual order, there are poor and rich. As the poor ask charity of the rich, and cannot live without help from them, so also in the spiritual order the poor must have recourse to the rich. We are the spiritually poor, whilst the saints, and those who shine even in this present life by their faith and piety, are the spiritually rich. It is to them that we needy ones must have recourse. We must beg for their prayers that they may help us to become simple as children, that they may teach us spiritual wisdom, how to conquer sins, how to love God and our neighbour. May the saints of God pray for us, that we may become like unto them.

God's saints are near to the believing heart, and are ready in a moment to help those who call upon them with faith and love. For the most part we have to send, and sometimes we have to wait long, for earthly helpers, whilst we have neither to send, nor to wait long, for spiritual helpers: the faith of him who prays can place them close to his heart in a moment, and he will speedily receive, through faith, spiritual help.

At the end of your morning and evening prayers call upon the saints, so that seeing every virtue realised in them, you may yourself imitate every virtue. Learn from the patriarchs childlike faith and obedience to the Lord, from the prophets and apostles zeal for the glory of God and the salvation of men, from the holy bishops zeal to preach the word of God, from the martyrs and confessors firmness before the infidel and godless, from the ascetics to crucify your own flesh and its lusts, and from the unmercenary ones not to love profit, and freely to help the needy.

Trust in the intercession of the Mother of God, and of the angels and saints, is a form of Christian hope. Their intercession for us is powerful, both by the grace of Christ, and as a consequence of their own virtues. It is not in vain that we pray to them: through their prayers we trust to obtain mercy,

65

the forgiveness of sins, and salvation, as well as temporal blessings.

If I pray to God with wholehearted, lively and perfect faith, then I am not only near him, as a son living in the same house is near to his father, but I am also near to all the heavenly powers, to all the saints reigning in heaven; and they are no farther away from me than are the images before which I pray. Therefore it is an excellent custom to have in our houses images of the Lord, of his immaculate mother, of the archangels, guardian angels, and saints, and to pray before them; the nearness of the image to our bodily sight betokens the still greater nearness of the subject to our spiritual sight, armed with undoubting faith.

When we pray the ears of the Lord incline to our prayer. He is then—as he always is—as near to us as the image before which we stand, and indeed much nearer: he is close to our very heart. His presence near to us is as manifest as the visible image, and therefore the image does but visibly represent how near the Lord is to us, how he looks upon us, and hears us. And God's saints, in the Holy Ghost, are also as near to us as the Holy Ghost is near to us, *who is everywhere present, and filleth all things, whose house we are,* and in the Holy Ghost they see and hear us, in the same way as we see and hear people speaking to us. For it is only through the Holy Ghost that we see and hear anything at all.

God and the saints hear us when we pray just as men hear each other when talking among themselves, or as people in church hear the preacher, or soldiers the voice of their commander, with this difference, that God and the saints hear our prayers incomparably better and more perfectly, because, when we hear the words of an ordinary man, we do not know what is in his heart and thoughts, and it may happen that he says one thing when he has quite another in his heart.

You do not understand how the saints in heaven can hear us when we pray to them? How do the rays of the sun descend from heaven to us, lighting the whole earth, and everything on it? The saints are in the spiritual world as the rays of the sun in the material world. God is the eternal life-giving sun, and the saints are the rays of the sun. As the eyes of the Lord are constantly looking upon earth, and those upon earth, so also the eyes of the saints cannot but follow the provident gaze of the Lord.

The heart is the eye of the human being; the purer it is, the quicker, farther and clearer it can see. But with God's saints this spiritual eye is refined, even in this life, to the highest degree of purity possible for man, and after their death, when they are united to God, it becomes, through God's grace, able to see yet more clearly and widely. Thus the saints see our spiritual needs, they see and hear all who call upon them with a whole heart, those who fix the eyes of their mind straight upon them, undarkened and undimmed by unbelief or doubt.

It is so easy to converse with the saints. It is only necessary to purify the eyes of the heart, to fix them firmly upon a saint known to you, and to pray for what you want—and you will get it.

When your faith in the Lord, whether in health or in sickness, in prosperity or poverty, whether at any time during this life, or at the moment of leaving it, grows dim, from worldly vanity or from illness and the terrors and darkness of death, then look with the eyes of your heart and mind upon the companies of the saints. See how, both during their earthly life and at the time of their departure from it, they looked unceasingly to God, and died in the hope of the resurrection unto life eternal—and strive to imitate them. These living examples, so numerous, can strengthen the wavering faith in the Lord and the future life of each and every Christian.

Those Christian communities who do not venerate the saints and do not call upon them in prayer lose much in devotion and in Christian hope. They deprive themselves of the great strengthening of their faith by the examples of men like unto themselves.

Watch yourself continually, that spiritual life and wisdom may not dry up within you. Think oftener upon what you read, or sing, or hear, in church, or sometimes at home. Live as the saints lived, by their prayers, wisdom and virtues; in meekness, humility and gentleness, not sparing yourself, but renouncing yourself, your rest, ease and enjoyment, for the love of God and your neighbour, in patience, courage and struggle—have their faith, hope and love.

A Christian ought to meditate upon things above, upon heaven, where Christ is, and not to cling to the corruptible blessings of the world: this is the concern of the heathen. But we attach ourselves passionately to all earthly pleasures and things. We pervert our life by withdrawing ourselves from the example set us by the Lord, the apostles, the martyrs, the confessors, the unmercenary ones, and all the saints. They were not of this world, but we are of this world; we lead a life according to our own ideas, not a Christian life.

The holy angels and other heavenly powers are full of pure, holy life, of unbroken peace, of unchangeable vigour, of eternal courage and strength, of indescribable beauty, light and wisdom; of the purest love for God and men, in a perfect fellowship; of divine light and enlightenment. Such also are the holy angels our guardians. But Christians who become worthy of attaining to the future life and to the resurrection from the dead will be equal to the angels, according to the word of the Lord himself. Let us therefore zealously strive after that life—unending, unchanging, untroubled.

All the saints in heaven, and all true Christians on earth, are *one body and one spirit;* this is why the prayer of believers is heard so easily, so speedily, so truly, in heaven, and why there is so much to be hoped for from calling upon the saints. But in order that our prayers should always be speedily and easily heard by the saints, we must have their spirit—the spirit of faith and of love for God and our neighbour, the spirit of meekness, humility, abstinence, purity and chastity, brave valiant, thirsting after righteousness, the spirit of compassion— heavenly, and not earthly.

He who prays to the Lord, to the Mother of God, to the angels and saints, must first of all endeavour to amend his heart and his life, and afterwards to imitate them, as it is written, *Be ye therefore merciful, as your Father also is merciful,* and again, *Be ye holy, for I am holy.* Those who pray to the Mother of God must imitate her humility, her unimaginable purity, submission to the will of God and patience. Those who pray to the angels must ponder upon the higher life, and strive to become truly spiritual, gradually laying aside all the lusts of the flesh, and striving for ardent love to God and their neighbour. Let those who pray to the saints imitate them in their love for God, and their contempt for the world, their prayers, abstinence, unselfishness, patience in sickness, sorrows, and misfortunes, their love for their neighbour. Without such imitation our prayer will be as useless as beating the air.

VI

THE HELP OF THE CHURCH ON EARTH

ONE

The Church of God

Your soul seeks true life and its natural food. The food of the mind is truth; the food of the heart is peace and blessedness; the food of the will is lawfulness. Go to the Church; she will give you all this in plenty, for she possesses it superabundantly. She is *the pillar and ground of the truth,* because in her is the Word of God, manifesting the origin of all things—the origin of the human race, how man was created after the image and likeness of God, how he fell, and has been restored through the Redeemer of mankind; in her also is revealed the means of salvation, faith, hope and love. She affords us peace and blessedness through her divine service, above all through the sacraments. She calls us: *Come unto me, all ye that labour and are heavy laden, and I will give you rest.* She teaches us the true way which leads to eternal life—the way of God's commandments.

We ought greatly to honour the Church, venerate her holiness, her antiquity, her unshaken firmness, her divinely enlightened wisdom and spiritual experience, her soul-saving commandments and ordinances, her divine services, sacraments and rites.

How can we do other than respect the Church, even if only for having saved in her bosom an innumerable multitude of people, translating them into the abode of eternal peace and joy, forgetting them not, even after death, but remembering them until now upon earth, praising and glorifying their virtues as her true children? Where will you find a more grateful friend, a more tender mother?

May Christians attach themselves wholly, with all their hearts, to the Church of Christ, that in her they may be firmly established unto the end of their days on earth. May they all be zealous to fulfil her commandments and ordinances, and in her may they obtain eternal salvation through Christ Jesus our Lord.

TWO

The House of God

The Church, through the ordering of the church building and her divine service, acts upon the whole man, educates him wholly: acts upon his sight, hearing, smelling, feeling, taste, imagining, mind and will, by the splendour of the images, and of the building in general, by the fragrance of the incense, by the veneration of the gospels, cross and images, by the singing, and by the reading of the scriptures.

The source of every true joy, of all true calm and peace of conscience, of cleansing, of spiritual and bodily healing, the source of spiritual power and boldness, flows in the church—theatres and other worldly distractions and consolations can never replace that which a true Christian receives in the church, where God himself comforts the souls of those who believe, and whose hearts are turned to him, as a mother comforts her child. It is from the church, also, that our departed ones receive consolation and solace, cleansing from their sins, and forgiveness.

Truly the church is heaven upon earth; for where the throne of God is, where the aweful sacraments are celebrated, where the angels serve together with men, ceaselessly glorifying the Almighty, there is truly heaven. And so let us enter into the house of God, with the fear of God, with a pure heart, laying aside all vices and every worldly care, and let us stand in it with faith and reverence, with understanding attention, with love and peace in our hearts, so that we may come away renewed, as though made heavenly; so that we may live in the holiness natural to heaven, not binding ourselves by worldly desires and pleasures.

In the church is accomplished the mystery of cleansing from sins. Reverence, therefore, the place where your soul is cleansed from all impurity, where you are reconciled to God, and are endowed with the true life of the Spirit.

How ardently we should love the house of God, how we should adorn it! So do, indeed, all who recognise its value; and the Church prays for them, saying *Let us pray for them that, with faith, reverence, and fear of God, enter herein;* and further, *Let us pray for them who bring forth the fruit of good works in this holy and venerable temple;* and again, *Hallow them that love the beauty of thine house; do thou by thy divine power exalt them unto glory.*

The adornment of holy things elevates our souls to God, and is therefore not merely not wrong, but positively holy and edifying, as also are sacred music, the fragrance of incense, the magnificence and splendour of the ornaments of the church building and its vessels. All these, destined to glorify God and to arouse devout feelings, are not sinful, but holy.

THREE

Common Prayer

Both public and private prayer are necessary in order that we may lead a truly Christ-like life, and that the life of the spirit should not become extinct in us. It is indispensable that we should attend divine service in church with faith, zeal and understanding, just as it is indispensable to provide a lamp with fuel or power if it is to burn and not to go out.

What does holy Church instil in us by putting into our mouths during prayer, both at home and in church, prayers addressed not by a single person, but by all together? She instils in us constant mutual love, in order that we should always love one another as our own selves—in order that, imitating God in three Persons, constituting the highest Unity, we should ourselves be one formed of many. *That they all may be one, as thou, Father, art in me, and I in thee, that they also may be one in us.* Common prayer on the part of all teaches us also to share the things of earth with others, to share our needs, so that in this life also we may have all things in common and as one—that is, that mutual love should be evident in everything, and that each of us should use his ability for the good of others, not hiding his talent in the ground, that he should not be selfish and idle. If you are wise, give advice to the foolish; if you are educated, teach the ignorant; if you are strong, help the weak; if you are rich, help the poor.

By means of its divine service, the Orthodox Church educates us for heavenly citizenship, by teaching us every virtue, by purifying and hallowing us, and making us godly, through the sacraments, and by giving *unto us all things that belong unto life and godliness.* Therefore it is urgently necessary for us intelligently, reverently and willingly to assist at the divine services of the Church, particularly on festivals, and to make use of the sacraments of penitence and holy communion. But those who withdraw themselves from the services of the Church become the victims of their vices, and are lost.

The Church offers us prayers by means of which we can easily incline the Lord to be merciful to us and to bestow upon us every good gift.

Where two or three are gathered together in my name, there am I in the midst of them. I reverence even two or three praying together, for in accordance with his promise the Lord himself is in the midst of them. A numerous assembly I reverence still more. Collective prayer is speedily fulfilled when it is united and unanimous—*gathered together in my name.* The assiduous prayer of the Church for the apostle Peter ascended at once before the throne of the Lord, and the Lord sent his angel miraculously to deliver Peter from the prison. The unanimous prayer of the apostles Paul and Silas brought down upon them wonderful help from the Holy Spirit.

77

When you pray, attend steadfastly to the words of the prayer, feeling them in your heart. Do not withdraw your mind from them to any other thought. When praying during divine service, during the celebration of the sacraments, lay surely to your heart the very words of the Church's prayers.

Those who attend the divine service of the Orthodox Church must bear in mind that its purpose is to prepare us for the joyful service of God in heaven; that in serving God with the body, it is still more necessary to serve God with the soul and a pure heart; that in hearing divine service they must learn to serve God as those saints served him, whose lives, and works of faith, hope and love, we hear of during the service; that God should, above all, be served in deed and truth, and not only by words and the tongue.

During divine service be trustful, as a child trusts his parents. Be simple, trustful, undoubting, as a child, in godly matters. Cast all your care upon the Lord, and be entirely free from sorrow: *Take no thought how or what ye shall speak: for it shall be given you in that same hour what ye shall speak. For it is not ye that speak, but the Spirit of your Father, which speaketh in you.* Long ago has the Lord freed us from this care, having by his Spirit taught the Church what to say, how to pray, at divine service.

If during service your brother does anything irregularly, or negligently, do not become irritated with him, whether inwardly or outwardly, but be generously indulgent to his fault, remembering that you yourself commit many, many, faults, that you yourself are a man with every weakness, that God is long-suffering and all-merciful, and that he forgives you and all of us our offences time without number.

The sin of inattention is one to which we are greatly subject; we must not disregard it, but must repent of it. We give ourselves up to it not only at home, but in church as well. *Simon, Simon, behold, Satan hath desired to have you, that he may sift you as wheat: but I have prayed for thee, that thy faith fail not.* The causes of inattention are the Devil, and our manifold attachment to the things of this world; its reason is want of faith; the means to overcome it is fervent prayer.

Those who go to divine service after having eaten much, voluntarily lay upon themselves an unnecessary and harmful burden; they deaden the heart before prayer, and obstruct the access of holy thoughts and feelings to it.

FOUR

The Word of God

The Holy Scripture is the realm of Wisdom, Word and Spirit, of God in Trinity; in it he clearly manifests himself: *The words that I speak unto you, they are spirit, and they are life.* In the Holy Scripture we see God face to face, and ourselves as we are. Man, know thyself through the scriptures, and walk always as in the presence of God.

When you doubt the truth of anything described in holy scripture, then remember that all scripture is divinely inspired, as the apostle says, and that it is therefore true, and does not include any false persons, fables and tales, although it includes

79

parables which every one can see are not true narratives, but are written in figurative language.

If the truth of something has been revealed in the Word of God, has been investigated and expounded to us by the divinely enlightened mind of the saints, whom God has glorified, and has been recognised by the heart in its light- and life-giving effects, then it is a great sin—devilish pride of the intellect and heart—to doubt it and to be perplexed about it.

The writings of the fathers, also, express the Mind, Word and Spirit, of the Holy Trinity, in which the spirit of the more spiritually advanced of mankind partakes.

If you read worldly magazines and newspapers, and derive some profit from them, as a citizen, a Christian, a member of a family, then you ought still more and still oftener to read the Gospel, and the writings of the fathers; for it would be sinful in a Christian who reads worldly writings not to read divinely inspired ones. If you follow the events of the outer world, do not lose sight of your inner world, your own soul: it is nearer and dearer to you. To read only worldly magazines and newspapers means to live only with one side of the soul, and not with the whole soul, or to live only by the flesh, and not by the spirit. Everthing worldly will come to an end with the world itself. *And the world passeth away, and the lust thereof; but he that doeth the will of God abideth for ever.*

Of those who do not read the gospel, I would ask: Are you pure, holy, and perfect, without reading the gospel? Is it not needful for you to look in this mirror? Or is it that your soul is so deformed that you fear to look upon your deformity? *They looked unto him, and were lightened: and their faces were not ashamed.*

As you are aware, man, in his words, does not die. He is immortal in them, and they will speak after his death. I shall die, but I shall speak even after my death. How many immortal words are in use among the living, which were left by those who have died long ago, and which sometimes still live in the mouths of a whole people! How powerful is the word, even of an ordinary man! Still more so is the Word of God: It will abide throughout all ages, ever living, ever acting.

Be firmly convinced that every word, above all those pronounced during prayer, is realisable, remembering that the author of the word is God the Word, and that our God himself, worshipped in the Holy Trinity, is expressed by three words or names: the Father, the Word, and the Holy Ghost; that each and every word corresponds to a fact, and that every word can become fact and deed. Woe to those that speak idly, for they will have to answer for their idle speaking!

Every word of Holy Writ, every word of the divine liturgy, of the morning and evening services, every word of the sacramental rites and the other prayers, bears in itself the power corresponding to it, as does the sign of the life-giving cross. Such grace is present in every word of the Church on account of the personal incarnate Word of God, who is the Head of the Church, dwelling in the Church. Besides this, every truly good word bears in itself the power corresponding to it, owing to the all-filling simple Word of God. How attentively and reverently, with what faith, must we therefore pronounce each word! For the Word is the Creator himself, God, and through the Word all things were brought into existence.

FIVE

The Use of Images

My carnal nature needs images. Therefore we rightly and justly make images and reverence them. What else is man himself but a living image of the living God?

Can our nature do without an image? Can we recall to mind an absent person without representing and imagining him? Has not God himself enabled us to represent and to imagine? Images are the Church's answer to a crying necessity of our nature.

Images or symbols are a necessity of human nature in our present spiritually sensual condition; they explain visually many things of the spiritual world which we could not apprehend without images and symbols. It was for this reason that the divine teacher, the personal Wisdom through whom all things were created, the Son of God, our Lord Jesus Christ, often taught men by means of images or parables. It is for this reason also that in our Orthodox churches it is the custom to represent many things to the sight of the Christian by imagery; for instance, to represent the Lord himself, the immaculate Mother of God, the angels and saints, on images, in order that we may conform our lives, all our thoughts, words and deeds, to the image of the thoughts, words, and deeds of the Lord and his saints.

It is an excellent custom with Christians, and one pleasing to God, to have an image of the Saviour and to pray to him before it. This is a crying necessity of our soul. The Lord himself, with the love which is proper to him, desires to be formed in us, as the apostle says: *My little children, of whom I travail in birth again until Christ be formed in you;* and: *that Christ may dwell in your hearts by faith.* But how can I form Christ in my heart if I do not first represent him sensibly before my eyes?

We have images of the Saviour, the Mother of God, and others. The love of Christians for them, desiring always to bear their images in their thoughts and hearts, as well as our nature, which is both carnal and spiritual, has given rise to the necessity of representing them on icons, placing them in the most honoured parts of the house, as in our hearts or the chambers of our soul, and of reverencing them by bowing to them, first spiritually, and then bodily.

Imagery greatly influences the creative or active capacity of the human soul. It is commonly held, for example, that if during the time preceding the birth of her child a mother often looks upon the face or portrait of her beloved husband, then the child is born very like his father. In the same way, if a Christian often gazes with love and reverence upon the image of our Lord Jesus Christ, or of his immaculate Mother, or of one of his saints, the spiritual features of the one lovingly looked upon—meekness, humility, mercy, abstinence, and so forth—will be imprinted upon his soul. If only we were to contemplate the images, and above all the lives, of the Lord and his saints more frequently, how we should change, and rise from strength to strength!

To venerate images is of great benefit to us, for it corresponds with our nature, and with commonsense, as well as with the holy scriptures themselves, for there were images of the cherubim in Moses' tabernacle of the old covenant.

Reverence in every way images of living men, in order that you may duly reverence the image of God. For the image of the Lord Jesus Christ is the human image. He who does not respect the human image will not respect the image of God.

By reverencing icons, first, I reverence in them God, who has begotten before all worlds the Son, his living image, who clothed in matter the infinite thought of God the Father by creating the worlds and all creatures that were in the thought of God and man, created after the image and likeness of God; second, I honour in them the image of God incarnate; third, I honour in them myself, man made in the immortal divine image, called to be a partaker of the divine nature, to unity with the Lord, to be the temple of the Holy Spirit.

Icons replace the persons themselves whose names they bear. The images of the saints upon our icons represent to us the nearness in the spirit of God's saints, who live in God, and are always close to us in the Holy Spirit, through our hearty faith and prayer to them.

The omnipresent Lord is in this image or in that cross, as in the word of the gospel. His image on the icon or cross is only an outward appearance, while he himself is the inward substance—manifesting himself everywhere, in everything, and through everything, and in particular through the images and signs upon which his worshipful name is inscribed, or his likeness is drawn.

I gaze upon the icons in the church, and think upon how the Creator and Provider of all has honoured and adorned our nature. His saints shine with his light, they are hallowed by his grace, having conquered sin and washed away every impurity of body and spirit. They are glorious with his glory, they are incorruptible through his incorruptibility. Glory to God, who has so honoured, enlightened and exalted our nature!

It is impossible to represent and to think of the cross without love. Where the cross is, there is love. In church you see crosses everywhere and on everything, in order that everything should remind you that you are in the temple of the God of love, the temple of love crucified for us.

We have images in our houses, and venerate them, in order to show, amongst other things, that the eyes of God and of all the company of heaven are constantly fixed upon us, and see not only all our acts, but also our words, thoughts and desires.

Is it only for the adornment of your dwelling, as an ornament, that you hang up richly painted icons in your house, without turning to them with the heartfelt faith, love and reverence due to holy things? Ask your heart if it is so. Icons in houses or in the temple are not intended for show, but for prayer before them, for reverence, for instruction. The images of the saints ought to be our teachers at home and in church. Study their lives, engrave them upon your heart, and endeavour to bring your life into conformity with theirs.

God rests in the saints, and even in their names and their images. It is only necessary to use their images with faith, and they will work miracles.

The wonder-working images of the Mother of God, and of other saints, teach us to look upon every image as upon the saint himself or herself to whom we pray as living persons conversing with us, for they are as near to us as the images—indeed, nearer—if only we pray to them with faith and sincerity. It is the same with the life-giving cross. Where the cross, or the sign of the cross, is, there is Christ himself, his power and salvation, if only we make the sign of the cross, or worship the image of the cross, with faith.

I am incited to venerate images because I see manifested in them the power of God, saving the faithful and punishing unbelievers, just as I see and feel this same power in the sign of the Lord's cross, which is called life-giving by reason of its miraculous power.

How in accordance with the mind of God it is that we venerate the images! Heaven itself answers us from them, as in olden times the Lord answered from the mercy seat in the tabernacle; many of them shine by miracles.

The Lord keeps, not only *all the bones,* but also the images of the saints, not allowing them to corrupt and perish, through carelessness and neglect, but miraculously renewing them, as we know from accounts of the appearance of wonder-working images, above all those of the immaculate Mother of God, our Lady. So dear to God is the image of man, particularly that of a holy man, as a vessel of grace. Through such images he works miracles, and bestows invisible powers of healing and consolation.

If anyone would ask you why you pray to lifeless images, what profit you derive from them, say that we derive incomparably greater profit from them than we do from the kindest and most benevolent of living persons; say that blessed power and help for our souls always comes to us from them, saving us from sin and sorrow and sickness—above all from the images of the

Redeemer and of the Mother of God; say that one single look with faith upon them, as upon those who are living and are near to us, saves us from cruel torments, vices and spiritual darkness; say that if touching the Saviour's garment, and the garments of the apostles, could restore health to the sick, much more are the images of the Saviour and of the Mother of God able to heal believers of every affliction, in accordance with their faith in the Lord and in his Mother.

Both the Lord himself and his immaculate Mother continually prove to us, by means of miracles, both inward and outward, that our true veneration of his Mother, and his saints, and of the holy images, is pleasing to him, and profitable to us in the highest degree.

The holy angels and the saints of God are our best, kindest, truest, brethren and friends, so often helping us in circumstances in which no one on this earth can do so. As these brothers, who load us with benefits, are invisible, whilst we, on account of our corporality, wish to have them before our eyes, we have images of them; and looking upon these images we call upon them in our prayers, knowing that they have great boldness before God, to help us.

Kissing with the lips corresponds to kissing with the soul; and when we kiss holy things, we ought to kiss them with the soul and heart as well as with the lips.

SIX

Sacraments and Sacramentals

Considering our bodily nature, the Lord binds his presence himself, to some visible and tangible sign—for instance, in the sacrament of the eucharist he himself wholly takes up his abode in the bread and wine which are his Body and Blood; in that of penitence he acts through the visible person of the priest; in that of baptism through water; in that of chrism, through the chrism; in that of orders through the bishop; in matrimony through the priest and the crowns he himself crowns the bride and bridegroom; in the sacrament of unction through the oil. He unites his presence to the church, to the images, to the cross, to the sign of the cross, to his name, to the holy water, to the blessed bread, wheat and wine; but the time will come when his sacramental Body and Blood, as well as all other visible signs, will no longer be necessary to us, for we shall then *more truly partake of him in the nightless day of his kingdom,* instead of only through images and symbols.

Reverence with all the powers of your soul all the sacraments, and say to yourself in respect of every sacrament before the celebration or communion of it, "This is God's mystery—I myself am only the unworthy witness or partaker of it". Otherwise, our proud intellect even wishes to search out the mystery of God, and if unable to penetrate it, rejects it as not coming under its own small measure.

During the celebration of divine service and of the sacraments the servant of God should be firmly convinced that whatever he thinks and says will be accomplished. It is so easy for the Lord to fulfil our requests, to create or to change anything in accordance with our words. Let this conviction be as easy and natural to you as your breathing the air, as seeing with your eyes, as hearing with your ears.

In making the sign of the cross, believe and constantly remember that your sins are nailed to the cross. When you fall into sin, at once judge yourself sincerely, and make the sign of the cross upon yourself, saying, Lord, thou that nailest our sins to the cross, nail also this my sin to thy cross, and *have mercy upon me after thy great goodness;* and you will be cleansed from your sin.

Our Lord is present in the priest's blessing by the sign of the cross, for in this sign he himself appears and blesses. Hence the importance of the priestly blessing. And even our customary making of the sign of the cross also bears God's power, if only we make it with faith.

It passes understanding how Jesus Christ unites himself to the sign of the cross, giving it the wonderful power of driving out vices and driving away demons, and of calming the troubled soul. And in order that the unbelieving heart should not think that the sign of the cross and the name of Christ act miraculously by themselves, apart from, and independently of, Christ himself, this same cross and name perform no miracles, unless and until I see Jesus Christ with the eyes of my heart—that is, by faith—and believe with my whole heart all that he has accomplished for our salvation.

Those who touched the Saviour's garment were made whole. Why is it that, even now, those who employ holy water with faith are healed? Because the cross, immersed in water, with the prayer of faith, is as though it were the life-giving Lord himself. As the Saviour's garments were penetrated with his life, so also the water, in which the life-giving cross is immersed, is itself penetrated with life, and becomes a water of healing.

The fragrance of incense reminds us by analogy of the fragrance of virtue, and by contrast of the evil odour of sins, and teaches those who are attentive to inward feelings to avoid the stench of vices—of intemperance, fornication, malice, envy, pride, despair, and such-like, and to adorn themselves with every Christian virtue; the incense reminds us of the apostle's words: *For we are unto God a sweet savour of Christ. in them that are saved, and in them that perish: to the one we are the savour of death unto death; and to the other the savour of life unto life.*

The candles and lamps burning in church remind us of spiritual light and fire, as of the Lord's words: *I am come a Light into the world, that whosoever believeth on me should not abide in darkness;* and again: *I am come to send fire on the earth; and what will I, if it be already kindled?* and again: *Let your loins be girded about, and your lights burning; and ye yourselves like unto men that wait for the Lord, when he will return from the wedding; that when he cometh and knocketh, they may open unto him immediately;* and: *Let your light so shine before men, that they may see your good works, and glorify your Father, which is in heaven.*

Do not grudge burning a wax taper before the image of the Lord during prayer; remember that you burn it before Light inaccessible, before him who enlightens you with his light. Your candle is as though a burnt offering to the Lord. Let it be a gift to God from your whole heart. Let it remind you that you yourself should also be a burning and shining light. *He was,* says our Lord of John the Forerunner, *a burning and a shining light.*

I offer light to the Lord, in order that he may bestow the light of grace, spiritual light, upon me, that he may lead me from the darkness of sin into the light of the knowledge of God and of virtue; I offer fire that the fire of the grace of the Holy Ghost may be kindled in my heart, and that it may quench the fire of the vices of that miserable heart. I bring a light that I myself may become a light, burning and shining to all that are in the church.

It is well to place candles before the images. But it is still better if you bring as a sacrifice to God the fire of your love for him and your neighbour. It is well that the one should accompany the other. But if you place candles before the images, and have no love for God and your neighbour in your heart, if you are grasping, if you do not live in peace with others—then, your offering to God is useless.

I am an infirm, carnal, sinful man. I am not always able to bring to my Lord a heart burning with faith and love—but at least I bring, as a carnal, material man, a material gift as a gift to heaven, a lighted candle. May the Lord look down from heaven upon this little gift of my zeal, and may he give me more in return. He alone is rich, and enriches all, whilst I am poor and needy. He dwells amid light inaccessible. whilst I am in darkness. I am of little faith; may he grant me the gift of faith. I am poor in love; may he enrich my heart with this priceless heavenly treasure. I am powerless to do good; may he give me that power.

SEVEN

The Divine Liturgy

The divine liturgy is truly a heavenly service on earth, in which God himself, in a particular, immediate and most close manner is present and dwells with men, for he himself is the invisible celebrant of the service; he is both the offerer and the offering. There is on earth nothing higher, greater, more holy, than the liturgy; nothing more solemn, nothing more life-giving.

Great is the liturgy. In it there is recalled the life, not of some great man, but of God incarnate, who suffered and died for us, who rose again and ascended into heaven, and who shall come again to judge the whole world.

The liturgy is the continually repeated enactment of God's love to mankind, and of his all-powerful mediation for the salvation of the whole world, and of every member of the human race separately. It is the marriage of the Lamb, the marriage of the King's Son, in which the bride of the Son of God is every faithful soul, and the giver of the bride the Holy Ghost.

The liturgy is the supper, the table of God's love to mankind. Around the Lamb of God on the paten all are at this time assembled—the living and the dead, the holy and the sinful, the Church above and the Church below.

God has opened for us, in his Body and Blood, the source of living water, flowing into life eternal, and gives himself to be our food and drink, *that we might live through him*.

Why should it be cause for wonder if God himself, the Creator of all things visible and invisible, transforms, transmutes, entirely changes, bread and wine into his own immaculate Body and Blood? In the bread and wine the Son does not again become incarnate, for he is already incarnate, and this suffices unto endless ages; but he is incarnate in the very same flesh in which he was before incarnate, just as he multiplied the five loaves, and with them fed several thousand people. There is many a mystery in nature which my mind cannot grasp, although it has a concrete form, and exists, mystery or no. So also, in this sacrament of the life-giving Body and Blood it is a mystery to me how the bread and wine are changed into the Body and Blood of the Lord himself, but the mystery of the Body and Blood really exists, although I cannot understand it.

The holy sacraments are called the divine gifts because they are given to us by the Lord freely, for nothing, undeservedly on our part. Instead of punishing us for the numberless sins we commit every day, and giving us over to spiritual death, the Lord, in the holy mysteries, forgives us, and cleanses us from all our sins, hallows us, and grants peace to our spiritual powers, healing and health of soul and body, and every blessing, simply in accordance with our faith.

If the Lord gives us himself, in his divine mysteries, every day, ought we not absolutely to give freely, for nothing, perishable goods such as money, food, drink, clothes, to those who ask them of us? And how can we be angered with those who eat our bread for nothing, when we ourselves partake freely of the priceless and immortal food of the Body and Blood of the Lord?

It is necessary to assist at the liturgy with pure, prepared, elevated, souls, in order not to be amongst the number of those who, having no wedding garment, but a garment defiled by vices, were bound hand and foot, and cast out from the marriage feast into utter darkness. Whilst now, unfortunately, many do not even consider it necessary to assist at the liturgy at all, others go only out of habit, and go away in the same state of mind as that in which they came, without elevated thoughts, without a contrite heart, with an unrepentant soul, without the resolve to amend. Some stand in church irreverently, inattentively, without having prepared themselves at home by means of meditative prayer and abstinence; and many manage to eat and drink more than they should before service.

How we cling to earthly things! We do not wish to devote even one hour exclusively to God. Even during the divine liturgy we allow ourselves to think and dream of earthly things and fill our souls with images and desires of earthly things, sometimes, alas, even with impure images—when we ought to be praying ardently, to be meditating assiduously upon this great mystery, to be repenting of our sins, longing and praying to be cleansed, hallowed, enlightened, renewed and strengthened in the Christian life, and in the fulfilment of Christ's commandments; when we ought to be praying for the living and the dead, for the liturgy is a sacrifice of thanksgiving and propitiation, of praise and prayer.

When the Lord descended upon Mount Sinai the Hebrew people were ordered to prepare and cleanse themselves beforehand. In the divine liturgy we have an even greater event than God's descent upon Mount Sinai; here before us is the very face of God the lawgiver. When the Lord appeared to him in the bush on Mount Horeb, Moses was ordered to put off his shoes from his feet: but here God is manifested in a manner far greater than upon Horeb; there was only the type, here is the antitype himself.

EIGHT

Holy Communion

He that eateth my Flesh and drinketh my Blood dwelleth in me and I in him. As an infant borne in his mother's womb lives wholly by her, so also the Christian partaking of the Body and Blood of Christ dwells in Christ, as an infant in its mother's womb, and lives wholly by Christ. *As I live by the Father, so he that eateth me, even he shall live by me.*

Why is it wonderful that the bread and wine become the Body and Blood of Christ, and that Christ rests in them as the soul rests in the body? Why is it wonderful when the Devil nestles in a tiny germ in the heart of the infant, and grows stronger with the growth of the body, so that afterwards the infant is born with the Devil already concealed and nestling in its heart? What infinite goodness and wisdom the Lord has shown by giving us the most pure sacraments of his Body and Blood, and by the fact that we take them into the depth of our hearts—that is, where the Devil nestles, having the power of sin and *the power of death*—as a perfect antidote to bestow upon us life and holiness, and to drive away sin and death! As undoubtedly as the Devil and every sin often nestles in our hearts, so undoubtedly does Christ, the life-giver, our hallower, dwell in our hearts. He is mightier than the Devil. If the Devil still lives and works in our hearts through our attachments to earthly things, then how shall not Christ enter into our hearts, through faith and repentance, when it was created to be the temple of God? How shall not Christ enter into our hearts precisely in his Flesh and Blood? And cannot Christ dwell in the bread and wine, transforming them, and completely assimilating them to himself as his Flesh and Blood?

What is there to be wondered at in the Lord's offering you his Body and Blood as food and drink? He who has given you as food the flesh of the animals he created has finally given you himself as food and drink. He who fed you at your mother's breast, now feeds you with his own Body and Blood, in order that, as with your mother's milk you absorbed into yourself in infancy something of the spirit of your mother, so you may absorb into yourself, together with the Body and Blood of Christ the Saviour, his spirit and life. Or as in your infancy you were fed by your mother and lived by her—by her milk—so now, having grown up and become a sinful man, you are fed with the Blood of your Life-giver, in order that through this you may live, and grow spiritually into a man —a man of God, a holy man. In short, that as you were then your mother's son, so now you may become the child of God, brought up and fed upon his Body and Blood, and, above all, with his Spirit, for his Body and Blood are spirit and life; and that you should become an inheritor of the kingdom of heaven, for which reason you were created, and for which you live.

You who partake of the holy sacraments, know how most truly you are united to the Lord if you communicate worthily. What boldness you have towards the Lord and towards his Mother! What purity, then, you ought to have! What meekness, humility, gentleness, detachment from the things of earth! What a burning desire for the pure and eternal joys of heaven!

In order to communicate of the life-giving sacrament with undoubting faith and to defeat all the wiles and falsehoods of the enemy, represent to yourself that what is received by you from the cup is *He who is*—that is, he who alone exists of himself. If the disposition of your thoughts and of your heart be after this manner, then by receiving the holy sacrament you will obtain peace, joy, and new life, and will recognise in your heart that the Lord truly and really dwells within you, and you in him.

How long will it be before the holy sacraments of which we partake remind us that *we, being many . . . are one body;* and how long will there be no heartfelt unity among us, as members of the one body of Christ? How long shall we live in enmity one to another, envy each other, torment, grieve, fret, judge and abuse each other? When will the Spirit of Christ abide in us, the spirit of meekness, humility, kindness, love unfeigned, self-denial, patience, chastity, abstinence, simplicity and sincerity, of contempt for the things of earth, and complete and single-minded longing for those of heaven?

How can you receive the Body of Christ worthily, with faith and love, when you despise his members, or have no compassion upon them? All Christians are members of Christ, especially those that are poor. Love his members, have compassion upon them, and the Master will bestow his great

97

mercy plentifully upon you. And can any mercy be greater than that which he bestows upon us in the communion of his immaculate Body and Blood?

He who believes in the Saviour, and feeds upon his Body and Blood, has life eternal in himself; and this is why every sin causes him painful suffering and disturbance of heart. But those who have not life eternal in them drink wickedness like water, and do not suffer, because life eternal is not in their hearts.

He who comes to the holy cup with any vice in his heart, the same is a Judas, and comes to kiss the Son of Man flatteringly.

There are many who communicate of the Body and Blood of Christ insincerely, not with great love, but with their mouths and stomachs only, with little faith, coldly, with hearts attached to food and drink, or money, or inclined to pride, malice, envy, sloth; and far from him who is all love, holiness, perfectness, great wisdom and unspeakable goodness.

What I say of insincere prayer applies equally to the communion of the holy, immortal and life-giving sacraments. At first, a man communicates with lively faith, with love and devotion, but afterwards he surrenders to the continual attacks of the flesh and the Devil, and communicates hypocritically, not of the Body and Blood, but of bread and wine, in accordance with the thoughts of his heart. The essence of the sacrament, *the spirit and the life,* has no place in him: he is inwardly robbed by Satan. May God preserve us all from such communion, from such blasphemy. It is the same also with the sacrament of penitence.

It is needful for such persons to go deeper into themselves, to repent more thoroughly, and to think profoundly upon what prayer *is*, and what Holy Communion *is*. Coldness of heart towards God proceeds from the Devil, it is the coldness of hell. Let us, as children of God, love the Lord with a love that burns.

Satan often enters into us when we have communicated unworthily, and in every way tries to instil his lie in our hearts —that is, unbelief, for unbelief is a lie. The destroyer of men tries in every way to destroy us by his lying, and by various thoughts and desires, and having stolen into the heart in the form of unbelief or some vice, he manifests himself in a manner worthy of him, mostly by impatience and malice, and you see that he is in you; but you will not often rid yourself of him at once, for he usually takes care to close every outlet in your heart by unbelief, obduracy and others of his brood.

Fear and uneasiness proceed from unbelief. Consider their arising during communion as a true sign that by unbelief you are removing yourself from the Life contained in the chalice, and pay no attention to them. *Thy faith hath made thee whole*. And after lively faith in God's truth we always depart in peace; whilst, on the contrary, after unbelief, always without peace.

In partaking of the holy sacrament be as sure that you partake of the Body and Blood of Christ as you are sure that every moment you breathe air.

Value by its effects that greatest miracle of Jesus Christ, the Son of the living God, manifested when we partake with faith of his divine sacraments. What is the miracle? The access of peace and life to your heart, killed by sin, which is so apparent after the uneasiness of heart and the spiritual deadness that often precedes communion. Never consider it from habit as anything ordinary or unimportant: by such thoughts you will incur the wrath of God, and you will not enjoy peace nor feel renewed life after communion. By the most lively and heartfelt gratitude for the holy and life-giving sacrament you will obtain Life from the Lord, and your faith will increase more and more.

If with faith you receive the holy sacraments, you will see that they will bring forth in your spiritual powers deep peace, with a wonderful sense of joy and freedom. The Lord loads us with benefits according to the measure of our faith; the Body and Blood give life to the believer's heart, according to the measure of its preparedness.

Most blessed, full of life, is the man who communicates of the holy sacraments with faith and heartfelt repentance for his sins. This we may truly feel, and the contrast is also manifest: if we approach the holy cup without sincere repentance for sin. and with doubt, then Satan enters into us, and dwells in us, destroying our soul, and this, too, is most perceptible.

In preparing for Holy Communion let us fear hardened insensibility to our sins; let us fear the pride of our hearts, which says, 'I am not sinful; I do not need any forgiveness of sins' or else, 'My sins are trifling, they are only human ones'—as though it were necessary that they should be devilish!—or, 'I do not feel amiss living in my sins'. This is the pride of Satan and it is Satan himself who speaks these words in our hearts.

Let us feel deeply, with our whole hearts, our innumerable wickednesses; let us mourn them from the very depths of our souls; let us shed contrite tears for them, that we may move to mercy the Master whom we have angered. Let us not in the least seek to justify ourselves like the Pharisees, the hypocrites, *for in thy sight,* it is written, *shall no man living be justified,* and we can only move God to be merciful to us by sincere repentance for our sins.

Let us put aside indifference and coldness; let us labour unto the Lord with a fervent spirit. Do not let us forget that we have now come to seek mercy of the Master of our lives, our righteous Judge, for the past period of our sinful lives. Is this, then a time for coldness and indifference, which are not approved of even in social intercourse, in our relations with our fellow-men? Ought not our soul, on the contrary to be turned into a spiritual fire, and pour itself forth in tears of most heartfelt repentance?

O my God, my God! Our sins have literally increased beyond the number of the hairs of our heads, above the number of the grains of sand of the sea, and yet we do not feel them, we are indifferent to them; even, we do not cease to love them. *If thou, Lord wilt be extreme to mark what is done amiss, O Lord, who may abide it?* May the Lord grant unto us all a contrite spirit and a humble heart, that we may offer to him true penitence. Amen.

Some believe that all they have to do before God is to read all the appointed prayers, without paying attention to the preparedness of their hearts for prayer, nor to inward amendment. In this way, for instance, many read the prayers appointed before Holy Communion; whilst at this time we should, above all, look to the amendment and preparedness of the heart to receive the holy sacrament. If your heart is right in your bosom; if, by God's mercy, it is ready to meet the bridegroom, then, thank God, it is well with you, even though you may not have succeeded in reading all the appointed prayers. *For the kingdom of God is not in word, but in power.*

Obedience to our mother the Church in everything is right; and if it is possible for one *to receive* prolonged prayer, let him pray at length. But *all men cannot receive this saying.* If long prayer is not compatible with fervour of spirit, then it is better to say a short but fervent prayer. Remember that the one word of the publican, said from a fervent heart, justified him. God does not look at the multitude of words, but upon the disposition of the heart. The chief thing is lively faith with fervent repentance for sins.

VII

SIN AND THE FORGIVENESS OF SIN

ONE

The Devil and his Works

The Devil takes an enormous part in the sins of men. Therefore, let none consider himself cast away, even if he be a great sinner: his sins are greatly the fault of the Devil. Turn at once to Jesus Christ for forgiveness—he is *the Lamb of God, that taketh away the sin of the world.*

A man is sometimes too irritable and too evil to be so of his own accord; he becomes so through the most zealous endeavours of the Devil. Only watch yourself or others at the time of irritability and wickedness, when you yourself, or anyone else, would wish to destroy the person inimical to you, really or mentally; compare this state with that which follows it, and you will say to yourself, 'No, this seems quite a different man from him, who, not long ago, was so full of evil and rage; this man is the one *out of whom the devils were departed, sitting at the feet of Jesus, clothed and in his right mind.* In him there is not even a shadow of the former wickedness, the former foolishness!' Some deny the existence of evil spirits, but phenomena in human life such as this clearly prove it. Besides, a man subjected to irritability, and breathing malice, clearly feels the presence of a hostile evil power in his breast; it produces in the soul the opposite of that which the Lord says of his own presence, *My yoke is easy, and my burden is light.* By the presence of the evil spirit one is made to feel ill at ease and oppressed, both in body and soul.

Between God and myself, between my neighbour and myself, there often stands a dark, evil power. I know this by experience, surely, logically.

The Devil cunningly induces us—instead of arousing us against himself—to notice our neighbours' sins, to make us spiteful and angry with others, and to awaken our contempt towards them, thus keeping us in enmity with them, and with the Lord God himself. Therefore, we must despise the sins themselves, and not our brother, who commits them at the Devil's prompting, through infirmity and habit; we must pity him, and gently and lovingly instruct him, as one who forgets himself, or who is sick, as a prisoner and the slave of his sin.

Remember that the enemy incessantly seeks to destroy you, and attacks you at the time when you least expect it. His malice is infinite. Do not bind yourself by self-love and sensuality, lest they take you an easy prisoner.

Know ye not your own selves, how that Jesus Christ is in you, except ye be reprobates? Truly, Christ dwells in me. Meanwhile, I have until now been a reprobate; I did not think, I was not firmly convinced, that the Lord is in me. It is he, the All-holy, that is so sensitive in me to the slightest impurity of heart; it is he who incites me to drive away from my soul the very germ of sin in the heart. But alas, Satan also is there, ready to devour me at every step, and contest with God for me.

The Devil generally enters into us through a single lying idea, or a single false thought, or a single sinful desire of the flesh, and from this beginning he works in us and troubles us. Cannot, therefore, the Lord of all spirits enter into us through a single thought, through true and holy love, and abide with us, and be everything to us? And therefore pray

106

undoubtingly; that is, simply, in the simplicity of your heart, without a doubt; it ought to be as easy to pray as to think.

God does not tolerate the slightest momentary impurity in you, and peace—God himself—leaves you at once if you admit any impure thought into your heart. And you become the abode of the Devil if you do not at once renounce the sin. So that at every sinful thought, and still more at every sinful word and deed, we must say 'this is the Devil'. Whilst at every holy and good thought, word and deed, we should say, 'This is God'.

Malice or the like that has taken root in your heart has a tendency—in accordance with the infallible law of evil—to discharge itself outwardly. This is why one usually says of an evil or angry man that he has vented his anger upon some person or object. It is the worst of evil that it does not rest in the heart, but attempts to diffuse itself outwardly. From this it is evident that the author of evil is himself great, and rules over a great territory.

There is no doubt that in the hearts of many people the presence of the Devil manifests itself by a kind of spiritual languor, exhaustion and sloth towards every good and useful work, especially works of faith and piety requiring attentiveness and soberness of heart, and towards spiritual work in general. Thus he strikes the heart with languor and the intellect with dullness during prayer, with coldness and indolence when it is necessary to do good— for instance, to have compassion upon those who suffer, to help those who are in need, to comfort those who are in sorrow, to teach the ignorant, to guide the erring and wicked into the way of truth. We must constantly watch our heart, drive away from it slothfulness and unfeelingness, and see that it always burns with faith and love for God and our neighbour, and is ever ready for every kind of labour and self-sacrifice for the glory of God and the salvation of our neighbour. *Not slothful in business; fervent in spirit; serving the Lord.*

The Devil also manifests his presence in our hearts by unusually violent irritation. We sometimes become so sick with our own self-love that we cannot endure even the slightest contradiction, any spiritual or material obstacle—cannot bear a single harsh word. But then is the very time for endurance, when the waters of malice and impatience reach the depths of our souls. What will become of a man when the Devil lets in upon him the floods of his temptations and blows upon him with the wind of his snares? If the Christian stands firmly upon the rock, Christ, then he will not fall; but if he stands upon the sand of his own sophistry and passions, then great will be his fall.

When you feel that there is no peace in your heart, through an undue care for anything earthly or worldly, and that the heart also breathes irritability and malice, be at once on your guard, and do not let your heart be filled with this devilish fire. Pray fervently, and strengthen your heart by the power of God. Be firmly assured that the evil is kindled in your heart by the enemy.

Sometimes, just when we begin to delight in the Lord, the enemy at once, himself or through human agents, brings the greatest sorrow upon us. Such is the lot of those who labour in this life for the Lord. For instance, you have just found peace and joy in the cup of the Lord, and at once after the service you are sorely tempted, and thereby afflicted. Even at the very cup the enemy sets snares for you, and disturbs you by thoughts which you must fight, or else, knowing that you have wished for a long, long time to find rest in God, the enemy will not allow it. As long as the old man lives, and is not dead within us, until then much sorrow must befall us from the struggles between the old man and the new.

At the approach of a great festival you must watch yourself with particular care. The enemy endeavours beforehand to chill your heart towards the subject, the event, celebrated; so that you will not honour it by whole-heartedly considering its reality. He acts upon us through the weather, or through the food and drink we have taken, or through his own arrows, thrown plentifully at the heart and inflaming the entire man, at which time evil, impure and blasphemous thoughts occur to us, and we feel thoroughly averse to the solemnity. We must overcome the enemy by forcing ourselves to meditate and pray devoutly.

The Devil is in the habit of attacking us when we are in straitened circumstances.

We are *a reed shaken with the* Devil's *wind*. The Devil breathes his blasphemy into our hearts and at once we are shaken by it. We are disturbed, depressed, when we ought to despise his every blasphemy, not take any notice of it, looking upon it as a mirage.

TWO

Sin in General, and its Cure

Remember that by every sin, by every attachment to anything worldly, by every displeasure and animosity towards your neighbour, by anything carnal, you offend the Holy Ghost, the Spirit of peace and love, the Spirit who draws us from things earthly to things heavenly, from the visible to the invisible, from the corruptible to the incorruptible, from the temporal to the eternal, from sin to holiness, from vice to virtue.

When you are threatened with temptation to sin, then represent to yourself vividly that sin is exceedingly displeasing to God. Mark that *sin, when it is finished, bringeth forth death,* because it kills the soul, because it makes us the slaves of the Devil, the destroyer of men; and the more we work for sin, the more surely we will be destroyed, the more difficult it will be to recover ourselves. Dread, therefore, every sin, with your whole heart.

To steer clear of sin, to seek forgiveness of sins actually committed, to strive to become holy; this above all else is desirable for man. For sins, such as pride, evil conduct towards others, distrust without cause, covetousness, avarice, envy, and the like, separate us from God, the Source of life, withdraw us from fellowship with other men, and plunge us into spiritual death.

When I sin, or indulge any undue longing for anything, then is the Lord far from me, not in respect to space, for at all times he fills everything, but in respect to my own spiritual withdrawal from him, to my own indifference towards him, in respect to my loss of his grace and presence in my heart, for his enemy, the Devil, then dwells in me.

Respect yourself as the image of God; remember that this image is a spiritual one, and be zealous to fulfil God's commandments, which re-establish his likeness in you. Be most careful not to break the least of his commandments, for this destroys your likeness to God, and brings you near to the likeness of the Devil. The more you transgress God's commandments, the more you will grow like unto the Devil.

God is not a God of torments and punishments. Our torments are the product of our own sins, and the work of the incorporeal fallen spirits. Therefore, if you suffer greatly, blame your sins and the Devil, but primarily yourself, because the Devil would not do you any harm if he did not find anything in you that he could fasten on to.

The root of every evil is a self-loving heart, or self-pity, self-sparing; it is from self-love, or excessive and unlawful love for oneself that all the vices proceed: coldness, insensibility, hard-heartedness towards God and our neighbour, wicked impatience and irritability, hatred, envy, avarice, despondency, pride, unbelief, gluttony, the love of money, vanity, slothfulness, hypocrisy.

Never pity yourself in anything, crucify yourself—your old man, nestling above all in the flesh—and you will strike at the root of all your vices. Bear patiently all that is unpleasant to your flesh; do not spare it, oppose it, and you will become a true follower of Christ. The whole wisdom of a Christian consists in wisely opposing the flesh in everything throughout life.

Every man on earth is sick with the fever of sin, with the blindness of sin, and is overcome with its fury. As sins consist mostly of malice and pride, it is necessary to treat everyone who suffers from the malady of sin with kindness and love. This is an important truth, which we often forget. Very often we act in the opposite manner: we add malice to malice by our anger, we oppose pride to pride. Thus, evil grows within us, and does not decrease; it is not cured—rather it spreads.

The mode of curing spiritual sickness differs entirely from the mode of curing bodily sickness. In the latter case one must concentrate upon the malady; the tender part must be treated by softening means—warm water, compresses, and so forth. But it is not so in the case of spiritual sickness; so if you are spiritually sick, strike the malady, crucify it; do not in any wise indulge it, do not cherish it, do not warm it; do the reverse of what it asks.

We sin in thought, word and deed. In order to become pure images of the most Holy Trinity we must strive that we be holy in thought, word and deed.

Sins of thought are not an unimportant matter for the Christian, because all that is pleasing to God in us is comprised in thoughts, for the thoughts are the beginning from which the words and deeds proceed. Words are important, because they either benefit those who hear them, or are corrupt and tempt others, perverting their hearts and thoughts; deeds still more so, because examples act more powerfully than anything upon people, inciting them to imitate them. The Lord is so holy, so simple in his holiness, that one single evil or impure thought deprives us of him, who is the peace and light of our souls.

If we took good note of the consequences of our sins and of our good works, how careful we should be to shun sin, and how zealous in all that is good. For we should then see clearly that every sin not eradicated in time becomes strengthened by habit, becomes deeply rooted in a man's heart, and some-times troubles, torments, and wounds him until death, be-coming so to say, awakened and revived in him every time he commits it, reminding him of the sins formerly committed, and in this way defiling his thoughts, emotions and con-science. Whilst on the contrary every good action done at any time sincerely, disinterestedly or habitually, gives joy to our heart and comfort to our life, in the knowledge that we have not spent our life entirely in vain, sinful though it be, that we are men and not beasts; that we are created after the image of God, and that there is a spark of the divine light and love in us; that, although they are but few, our good works will balance our evil ones in the scales of God's incorruptible righteousness.

How corrupt I am become through sin! Anything bad, evil, impure, at once enters into my thoughts and is felt in my heart whilst anything good, right, pure, holy, is often only thought and spoken of, and not felt. Woe unto me, for as yet evil is nearer to my heart than good. Besides this, we are at once ready to do evil as soon as it is thought of or felt, and we do it quickly and easily if we have no fear of God, whilst *how to perform that which is good I find not* the power within me, and the intended good work is often put off indefinitely.

It is time that we should understand the Lord, time that we should understand what he requires of us, a pure heart. This should be our common problem, to bring Christ to dwell in our hearts through faith.

When the heart is pure, then the whole man is pure; when the heart is unclean, the whole man is unclean: but the saints acquired pure hearts by fasting, vigilance, prayer, by meditating, and reading the Word of God, by martyrdom, by labour and sweat; and the Holy Ghost abode in them, cleansed them from every impurity, and hallowed them eternally. Strive above all, then, for the cleansing of your heart. *Make me a clean heart, O God.*

Do not neglect anything in the spiritual life; do not consider anything unimportant: it is through little sins that the Devil leads us to greater ones.

The sin to which you do not consent is not imputed to you—for instance, involuntary wandering of the thoughts during prayer, impure and blasphemous thoughts, or involuntary malice, which we zealously combat, avarice which we resist—all such are attacks of the spirit of evil. Our duty is to endure, to pray, to humble ourselves, and to love.

THREE

Self-examination

Sin closes the spiritual eyes. The thief thinks that God does not see; the fornicator, giving himself up to impurity, thinks that God does not see; the covetous, the greedy, the drunkard, all think that they can hide themselves, that God does not see. But God sees, and judges. *I was naked, and I hid myself—* so, in effect, says every sinner, hiding himself from the omnipresent God.

The greatest continual error of our heart, which we ought unceasingly to fight throughout our life, morning, noon and night, is the secret thought that we can be anywhere and at any time without God, outside him even for a single moment.

However far I may let my thoughts and imagination run, God is there before me, and I inevitably finish my course in him, ever having him as the witness of my ways. His *eyes are open upon all the ways of the sons of men. Whither shall I go then from thy Spirit, or whither shall I go then from thy presence?*

Conscience in men is nothing else but the voice of the omnipresent God moving in the heart—the Lord who knows all: thoughts, desires, intentions, deeds; past, present and future.

Watch your heart throughout your life; examine it, listen to it, and see what prevents it from uniting itself with the Lord. Let this be your supreme and constant study, and with God's help you will easily observe what estranges you from him, and what draws you to him and unites you to him. It is the evil spirit more than anything else that stands between our hearts and God; he estranges us from God by the several vices, or by the desires of the flesh, and by worldly pride.

Examine yourself oftener; see where the eyes of your heart are looking. Are they turned towards God and the life to come, towards the perfect, blessed, resplendent and holy powers of heaven? Or are they turned towards the world, towards earthly blessings: food, drink, dress, abode; to the sinful vanity, works and pastimes of men?

FOUR

Repentance

To repent means to feel in our hearts the falsehood, the madness, the wickedness of our sins; it means to acknowledge that we have offended, by them, our Creator, our Lord, our Father, our Benefactor, who is infinitely holy, and infinitely abhors sin; it means to desire with the whole soul to amend and to atone for our sins.

Why does not the sinful soul obtain forgiveness of its sins before it feels all the foolishness, destructiveness and falsity of them from the whole heart? Because the heart is our soul; as it committed the sins, finding them at the time pleasant and plausible, therefore it must now repent of them and recognise them as leading to destruction, as entirely wrong. This repentance is accomplished painfully in the heart, as the desire to sin is also usually in the heart.

Amidst all your worldly pleasures, man, the greatest misfortune hangs over you. You are a sinner; you are God's enemy; you are in great danger of losing eternal life, particularly if you live negligently, if you do not bring forth works meet for repentance. The wrath of God hangs over you, particularly if you do not appease by your prayers, penitence and amendment the God whom you have offended. This is not time for pleasures, but rather for tears; your pleasures should be rare, and principally such as are afforded spiritually in the feasts of the church.

How many of us have the feeling of sonlike love to God? Dare many of us *boldly and uncondemned call upon the God of heaven as Father and say, Our Father* ... ? On the contrary is it not true that there is no such sonlike love in our hearts, which are deadened by attachment to the things of this world? Is not our Heavenly Father far from our hearts? Is it not rather an avenging God that we should represent to ourselves, we who have withdrawn ourselves from him into a far-away land? Yes, by our sins we are all of us worthy of his righteous anger and punishment, and it is wonderful how long-suffering and forbearing he is to us—that he does not strike us as he struck the barren fig-trees. Let us hasten to call forth his mercy by repentance and tears. Let us enter into ourselves; let us carefully consider our unclean hearts, and when we see how manifold is the filthiness which we oppose to the working of the divine grace, we shall acknowledge that spiritually we are dead.

Repent ye: for the kingdom of heaven is at hand. Is at hand—that is, has come by itself. It is not necessary to seek for it long—it seeks us, our free inclination; that is, you yourself must repent with heartfelt contrition.

Penitence should be sincere, perfectly free, and not in any way forced by any particular time and habit, or by the person before whom the sinner confesses. Otherwise it would not be true penitence.

As our prayer consists principally of penitence and asking forgiveness for our sins, it must always be absolutely sincere and perfectly free, not contrary to our will, not forced out of us by habit and custom.

FIVE

Contrition

How we should sorrow from the depths of our hearts at our hardened lack of feeling; how we should lament it before the Lord! If we do so, it will pass away, and the heart will be made warm and tender, and once more able to contemplate with feeling the things of the spirit.

If in any way you sin before God (and we all sin greatly every day), at once say in your heart with faith in the Lord, who hears you, the psalm *Have mercy upon me, O God, after thy great goodness,* humbly and with feeling acknowledging your sins. Say the whole psalm with a whole heart. If it does not take effect the first time, repeat it still more earnestly, still more feelingly, and then the saving peace of the Lord shall soon descend upon your soul. Be ever contrite; this is the true and proven remedy for sin. If you still do not obtain relief, blame yourself. It shows that you have prayed without contrition, without humility of heart, without a strong desire to obtain forgiveness of your sins from God; it shows that you are not deeply grieved at your sin.

When you stand praying, burdened with many sins, and overpowered by despair, begin to pray with hope, with a fervent spirit, and remind yourself that *the Spirit itself maketh intercession for us with groanings which cannot be uttered*. When you recall with faith this work of the Spirit of God within us, then tears will flow from your eyes, you will feel, in your soul, peace *and joy in the Holy Ghost,* and you will cry in your heart *Abba, Father!*

It is necessary to wash, in order to cleanse ourselves from dirt, and prayer—above all, tearful prayer—is the washing by which we cleanse ourselves from spiritual filth, that is, sin.

Streams of tears are necessary to wash away the inveterate filthiness of sin. How it clings! How malignant it is!

The Lord turned and looked upon Peter . . . and Peter went out, and wept bitterly. And even now, when the Lord looks upon us we weep bitterly over our sins. Our tears during prayer mean that the Lord has looked upon us, he whose regard gives life to everything, and examines the heart. Sometimes we do not see any outlet, any escape from our sins, and they torment us; on account of them the heart is oppressed with sorrow and weary; but *Jesus looks upon us,* and streams of tears flow from our eyes, and with the tears all the tissue of evil in our soul vanishes; we weep with joy that such mercy has suddenly and unexpectedly been sent to us.

Fervent, tearful prayer not only cleanses from sins, but also cures bodily weaknesses and diseases; it renews the whole of a man, and makes him, so to say, born again. I speak from experience.

SIX

Confession

Consciousness, memory, imagination, feeling, and will are helps to penitence. As we sin with all the powers of our soul, so penitence must be from the whole soul. Penitence in words only, without the intention of amendment and without the feeling of contrition, may be called hypocritical. Should the consciousness of sins be obscured, it must be cleared up; should the feeling be smothered and dulled, it must be roused; should the will become blunt and too weak for amendment, it must be forced: *The kingdom of heaven suffereth violence, and the violent take it by force.* Confession must be sincere, deep and full.

I am only the witness that I may bear witness before him of all thou tellest me. The priests will witness before the Saving Judge on the terrible day of judgment concerning sinners, whether they did or did not repent of these or those sins, and they who were penitent will be forgiven. But why is it necessary for God to have witnesses, when he himself knows everything. *He needed not that any should testify of man, for he knew what was in man.* Indeed they are not necessary to God, but they are necessary for us. It will be pleasant for us to see how the priests will bear witness concerning us, before angels and men, that we repented of our sins, condemned ourselves, expressed our loathing for sin, firmly resolved not to sin further.

It is absolutely necessary to confess at least once every year. The longer we go on without confessing, the worse it is for us, the more entangled we become in the bonds of sin, and therefore the more difficult it is to give account.

We ought to confess our sins more frequently, in order to strike and scourge the sins by the open avowal of them, and in order to feel a greater loathing of them.

He who is accustomed to give account of his life at confession will not fear to give an answer at the terrible judgment-seat of Christ. For this purpose was the mild tribunal of penitence here instituted, that we may give an answer without shame, having been cleansed and healed through penitence here below. This is the first motive for sincere confession.

A second motive is inner calm. The more sincerely we confess our sins, the more calm will the soul be afterwards. For sins are secret serpents, gnawing at the heart of a man, and never letting him rest; they are prickly thorns, constantly goring the soul, they are spiritual darkness.

Bear the sufferings of the operation so that you may be restored to health—I speak of confession. I mean that at confession you must declare *all* your shameful deeds to your confessor, without concealment, though it may well be painful, shameful, ignominious and humiliating. Otherwise the wound will remain unhealed, will continue to pain you, will undermine your spiritual health, and remain as a leaven for other spiritual weaknesses, or sinful habits or vices.

A priest is a spiritual physician. Show your wounds to him without shame, sincerely, openly, trusting and confiding in him as his son; for the confessor is your spiritual father, who should love you more than your own father and mother; for Christ's love is higher than any natural love. He must give an answer to God for you.

Why is our life so impure, so full of sinful habits? Because a great many conceal the spiritual wounds and sores which are the root of the trouble, and therefore it is impossible to apply any remedy to them.

He hath made him to be sin for us, who knew no sin, that we might be made the righteousness of God in him. Will you be ashamed after this to acknowledge any of your sins, whatever they may be, or to take upon yourself the blame for sin which you have not committed? If the Son of God himself was made sin for us, though he was sinless, then you, too, must accept blame for all sins with meekness and love, and accept blame humbly and submissively, even for those sins which you have not committed, for in truth you are guilty of all.

In this life we sin continually, and at the same time we are so self-loving that we cannot endure to be reproved for our sins and faults, above all before others; but in the future life we shall be reproved for them before the whole world. Bearing in mind this terrible judgment-seat, let us bear reproof here humbly and gently, and let us correct ourselves of all our sins, all our faults; above all, let us bear reproof from those in authority over us, and may the Lord teach them to reprove our faults not with malice, but with love and in the spirit of meekness.

As soon as you have told the Lord your sins, with a contrite heart, they melt away; as soon as you have sighed and sorrowed for them, they are no more. *Tell me thine iniquities, that thou mayest be justified*. As they came, so they go away. They are an illusion. As soon as you have recognised that they are an illusion, an absurdity, a madness; as soon as you have resolved to do aright in the future, God cleanses you of them, through his minister and the holy sacraments.

Bear in mind that for cleansing your heart from sin, you will get an infinite reward—you will see God. The work of cleansing the heart is difficult, for in the course of it we are greatly afflicted; and therefore the reward is great. *Blessed are the pure in heart; for they shall see God.*

SEVEN

Amendment

Firmly purpose in your soul to hate every sin of thought, word and deed, and when you are tempted to sin resist it bravely, and with hatred for it; only beware lest your hatred should turn against the person of your brother who gave occasion for the sin. Hate the sin with all your heart, but pity your brother, instruct him, and pray for him to the Almighty God, who sees us all, and examines our hearts and innermost parts.

Ye have not yet resisted unto blood, striving against sin. It is impossible not to fall often into sin unless you have a hatred of it implanted in your heart. Self-love must be eradicated. Every

123

sin comes from the love of self. Sin always appears or pretends to wish us well, promising us plenteousness and ease. *The tree was good for food, and it was pleasant to the eyes, and a tree to be desired to make one wise.* This is how sin always appears to us.

If you fall, rise, and you shall be saved. You are a sinner, you continually fall; learn also how to rise—be careful to acquire this wisdom, which consists in learning by heart the psalm *Have mercy upon me, O God, after thy great goodness,* inspired by the Holy Ghost to the king and prophet David, and in saying it with sincere faith and trust, with a contrite and humble heart. After your sincere repentance, expressed in the words of this psalm, the forgiveness of your sins shall at once shine upon you from the Lord, and your spiritual powers will be at peace.

For what purpose does the Lord add day after day, year after year, to our existence? In order that we may gradually put away, cast aside, evil from our souls, each one his own, and acquire blessed simplicity; in order that we may become truly gentle; in order that we may learn not to have the least attachment to earthly things, but as loving and simple children may cling with all our hearts, all our souls, and all our thoughts, to God alone, and so to love him, and our neighbour as ourselves. Let us therefore hasten to pray to the Lord, fervently and with tears, to grant us simplicity of heart, and let us strive by every means to cast out the evil from our souls.

EIGHT

Faith in Forgiveness

When you have sinned, and your sins torment you, then seek at once the only sacrifice for sins, eternal and living, and lay your sins before the face of that sacrifice. Do not think that you can be saved by your own efforts.

Christian hope is our hope in Christ, and in the eternal bliss promised us by him. He is the limit of our desires: *He shall save his people from their sins*. Many say, 'I should like to go to Paradise, but my sins will not let me'. Those who speak thus have no idea of Christian hope; they look upon their sins as upon a kind of indestructible wall. No; Christ Jesus has destroyed this very wall by his death upon the cross, and has opened God's Paradise to all who will repent.

When you pray that your sins may be forgiven, strengthen yourself always by faith, and trust in God's mercy, who is ever ready to forgive our sins after sincere prayer; and fear lest despair should fall upon your heart—that despair which declares itself by deep despondency and forced tears. What are your sins beside God's mercy, whatever they be, if only you truly repent of them?

It often happens that when a man prays he does not in his heart hope that his sins will be forgiven, counting them as though above God's mercy. For this reason he will not be forgiven, even though he shed rivers of involuntary tears; and with a sorrowful and oppressed heart he will depart from the God of grace, which is only what he deserves. Not to be sure of getting that for which you ask God is blasphemy.

NINE

Despair of Forgiveness

Who does not know how difficult it is, without particular grace from God, for a sinner to turn from the way of sin, which is so dear to him, into the path of virtue? How deeply sin takes root in the heart of a sinner, and in all his being—how it gives the sinner its own way of looking at things, by means of which he sees them differently from what they are in reality, and shows him everything in a kind of alluring light. It is for this reason that sinners very often do not even think of turning from sin, and do not consider themselves great sinners, because they are blinded by self-love and pride. And if they do consider themselves sinners, then they give themselves up to the most terrible despair, which overwhelms the mind with thick darkness, and greatly hardens the heart.

By means of the spirit of despondency the enemy has driven many from the narrow path of salvation on to the broad and smooth path that leads to destruction.

Even the saints of God were at times seized with diabolical despair and despondency. What therefore can we sinners expect? The enemy often wounds us by implanting in our heart wrath, shame and cruel despondency. We must turn to God continually; every moment we must be with him, in order that we may not be besieged with the wrath and despondency of the enemy.

There are other means of escaping from despair and despondency—the broad way of the world: if you give yourself up to worldly pleasures, despondency will leave you for a time, at least while the pleasures last. But afterwards you will be captivated by these pleasures; they will become a necessity to you, and you will find comfort and joy in them alone. May God preserve every Christian from finding his only way of escape from the despondency of the Devil through such means!

It is better to walk in the narrow path, to bear with despondency, and to seek frequent help and deliverance from the Lord Jesus Christ, who always gives joy to those labouring to save themselves for his sake, than to enter on the broad and smooth way of the world and purchase there, by means of the pleasures of the flesh, freedom from the spirit of despondency.

Never despair of God's mercy, no matter by what sins you may have been bound through the tempting of the Devil, but pray with your whole heart, with the hope of forgiveness; knock at the door of God's mercy, and it shall be opened unto you. Do not despair, then, whatever sins you have committed; only repent and confess them with a contrite heart and humble spirit.

You, sinner, who have fallen into the depths of evil, when you represent to yourself the multitude of your sins, and fall into despair and hardness of heart, remember that the

Heavenly Father sent his only-begotten Son, our Lord Jesus Christ, into the world to save you from your sins, and from the eternal condemnation which they merit. Turn then with faith to him, imploring him from the depths of your soul to wash away your sins by his all-cleansing blood, shed for us on the cross; turn zealously to repentance, confessing your sins before his priest as before himself, that you may be justified; after which, if the minister of penitence finds you prepared and fit, draw nigh to the holy cup, and you shall be cleansed from all your sins: peace shall flow into your soul like a river, and you shall be the son of the Heavenly Father, the son who *was dead and is alive again, who was lost and is found.*

If the Lord were not long-suffering, if he were not the lover of men, would he have borne with our great offences? Would he have been incarnate? Would he have suffered even unto death for you? Would he have given you his immaculate Body and Blood, upon which even the angels look with fear and trembling? Would he so many times have saved you from sin and spiritual death? Had it been otherwise, he would say: Be tormented, if you are so evil by nature; I will not deliver you after having delivered you so often before. But throughout our life he bears with our innumerable offences, and still he awaits our conversion. Glorify, then, his love and long-suffering. Imagine what it would have been like without him to save you. Horror and trembling fill the soul at the very idea of it. But impenitent sinners will indeed be overtaken by God's wrath *in the day of wrath, when the righteous judgment of God shall be revealed.*

Believe firmly that it is the wickedness of the Devil which is in you, and that your own wickedness will never conquer the unspeakable, infinite mercy of God. Great is the wickedness of the Devil in you, but the mercy of God is infinitely greater.

Therefore, in times of doubt, unbelief, blasphemy, malice, envy, avarice, covetousness, involuntary hypocrisy, entreat the Lord with hope, and be sure that his infinite goodness will incline him to have mercy upon you, if you turn from your wickedness.

VIII

THE SPIRITUAL WARFARE

ONE

The Nature of the Spiritual Warfare

What is holiness? Freedom from every sin, and the fulness of every virtue. This is only attained by a few zealous persons in this life, and that not suddenly, but gradually, by prolonged and manifold sorrows, sicknesses, and labours, by fasting, vigilance and prayer; and that not by their own strength, but by the grace of Christ.

Having Christ in your heart, fear that you may lose him, and with him the peace of your heart. It is hard to begin again; efforts to attach oneself afresh to him after falling away will be very grievous, and in many cases will cause bitter tears. Cling to Christ with all your might, hold fast to him, and do not lose boldness in approaching him.

Why is it that only the narrow way and narrow gate lead to life? Who makes the way of the chosen narrow? The world oppresses the chosen, the flesh oppresses them, the devil oppresses them; it is these that make our way to the kingdom of heaven narrow.

Both the spiritual and bodily powers of a man increase, and are perfected and strengthened, by exercise. By exercising yourself in good works or in conquering your vices and temptations, you will in time learn to do good works easily and with delight: and with the help of God's grace you will easily

133

learn to conquer your vices. If you cease praying, or pray seldom, prayer will be oppressive to you. If you do not fight your sinful habits, or only do so seldom and feebly, you will find it very difficult to fight them, and you will often be conquered by them; if you do not learn how to conquer them, they will give you no rest, and your life will be poisoned by them.

Those who are trying to lead a spiritual life have to carry on a most skilful and difficult mental warfare, a spiritual warfare, every moment throughout life; it is necessary that the soul should have every moment a clear eye, able to watch and notice the entrance into the heart of thoughts sent by the evil one, and to repel them. The hearts of such men must always burn with faith, humility and love; for otherwise the subtilty of the Devil finds an easy access to them, which is followed by a decline, or even by an entire loss, of belief, and afterwards by every possible evil, difficult to wash away, even by tears.

Strive in all things to oppose that which the bodiless enemy wishes you to do. He incites you to pride, to self-glory, and to judging your brother: you must humble yourself to the ground, to dust and ashes, judge yourself as severely as possible, and praise your brother in your heart. Should your brother, through the work of the enemy, behave towards you with pride and malice, you must behave towards him humbly and lovingly. If the enemy incites you to avarice, be generous, with a good will. Act thus in every similar circumstance, and God will give you abundant grace; this you will see for yourself, with your spiritual eyes. If you have not the inward strength to do this, through the great power of the enemy, then pray for it, in every season, in every hour, and the Almighty God will help you.

Oppose everything that the enemy suggests to you. He suggests that you hate those that offend you—you must love them;

bless those that curse you, and do not trouble those who take away your property, but give it away willingly. When you want to laugh, weep; when you feel despondent, endeavour to be glad; when you feel envious, rejoice at the prosperity of others; when you are inclined to contradict and disobey, agree and submit at once; when impure thoughts occur to you, be zealous for the purity of your heart, represent to yourself the high destiny of a Christian, made godly in Christ Jesus, and call to mind that our members are the members of Christ; when you feel proud, humble yourself; when spiteful, be particularly kind; when irritable keep calm; when mean, be generous; when distracted, at once close your feelings to all outward things, and meditate on the *one thing needful*; when you feel doubt or unbelief, call firm faith to your help, remind yourself of the examples of faith, of the miracles accomplished by faith, and so on. Do thus, and do not give way to the enemy; for all vice, every evil and foolish fancy, is of his imagining.

Do not fear the conflict, do not flee it. Where there is no struggle, there is no virtue; where faith and love are not tempted, it is not possible to be sure whether they are really present. They are proved and revealed in adversity, that is, in difficult and grievous circumstances, both outward and inward—during sickness, sorrow, or privations.

Sometimes the soul is surrounded and penetrated by a light, pleasant, warming and lifegiving breath, and we feel happy and are at peace; at other times the heart is touched by a heavy, deathly breath, bringing complete spiritual darkness. The first state proceeds from the Spirit of God, the second from the Devil. It is necessary to accustom ourselves to everything: as in the first case, not to grow conceited; so in the second, not to fall into despondency, but fervently to have recourse to God.

During the life of the Christian there are hours of inconsolable sorrow and sickness, when it seems that the Lord has completely abandoned and forsaken him, for there is not the least feeling of God's presence in the soul. Such are the hours in which the faith, hope, love, and patience of the Christian are tried. But better times will soon come to him. Soon the Lord will turn him again to joy, so let him not fall when tempted in this way.

Do not be despondent when the clouds of hell, each darker than the last, descend upon your soul; when infernal malice, envy, doubt, obstinacy and other vices rise up in your soul. Know surely that the gathering of these dark clouds upon your mental horizon is inevitable; but they are not always there, and they will not remain long—like dark clouds in the natural sky they pass over and disappear, and afterwards the mental atmosphere is clear again. As in nature, clouds in the sky there must be, and the darkening of the light of day, but the clouds are not constant, they soon pass away, and then the light of the sun shines forth again with renewed power.

Do not despond when fighting the incorporeal enemy, but even as you are afflicted and oppressed glorify the Lord, who has found you worthy to suffer for him, in resisting the subtilty of the serpent, and to be wounded for him at every hour; for had you not lived devoutly, and endeavoured to unite yourself to God, the enemy would not have attacked and tormented you.

We must trust in God in all temptations, in every desolate condition of the soul. The Lord will deliver.

TWO

The Armoury of the Spiritual Warfare

I myself am all infirmity and misery. God is my strength. To know this is to me the highest wisdom, making me blessed.

I am nothing without the Lord. I have really not one true thought or good feeling, and I can do no good work; without the Lord I cannot drive away from me any sinful thought, or any sinful feeling, or any inclination to vice. It is the Lord who accomplishes every good thing that I think, feel, and do. How boundless is the grace of the Lord acting in me!

What is grace? It is the blessed power of God, given to the man who believes and has been baptised in the name of Jesus Christ—the power that cleanses, hallows, enlightens, that helps us to do good, and withdraws us from evil, that comforts and encourages us in misfortunes, sorrows, and sickness, that is a pledge of the everlasting blessings, prepared in heaven for the chosen of God.

If anyone has in any way changed for the better, he has done so by the power of grace alone, Without grace you cannot conquer any sin, any vice; therefore, always ask help of Christ your deliverer. It was for this that he came into the world, for this that he suffered, died, and rose from the dead —in order to help us in all things, to save us from the power of sin, and from the force of our vices, to cleanse us from our

137

offences, to bestow upon us in the Holy Ghost power to do good works, to enlighten us, to strengthen us, to give us peace. You ask how you can save yourself when sin stands at every step, and you sin at every moment? The answer is simple: at every step, at every moment, call upon the Saviour, and you will save yourself and others.

It is evident that many live without grace, not recognising its importance and its absolute necessity, and that they do not seek it, although the word of the Lord says, *Seek ye first the kingdom of God and his righteousness.* Many live in plenty and ease, enjoy blooming health, eat, and drink with pleasure, walk, amuse themselves, write, or labour in this or that human activity, but they have not the grace of God in their hearts, that priceless treasure of the Christian, without which none can be a true Christian, and an inheritor of the kingdom of heaven.

The light of Christ enlightens all, even the heathen. *A light to lighten the Gentiles.* It shines even in the darkness of sin, but sinful human darkness, or, rather, the men living in the darkness of sin, do not understand it; they do not realise that the light which is in their souls is from Christ, and think that it is their own natural light.

Remember constantly that the light of your heart, and of your thoughts, comes from Jesus Christ. He is the light of our heart—a light not like that of the sun, which appears and disappears, and does not penetrate through any opaque substance, but leaves many things in darkness, and cannot enlighten a single soul in the darkness of sin; no, he is *the true Light which lighteth every man that cometh into the world.*

In order not to be in perpetual bondage to your vices and to the Devil, you must set yourself an object. Have it constantly before you, and endeavour to reach it, conquering all obstacles in the name of the Lord. What is this object? The kingdom of God, the divine palace of glory, prepared for believers from the creation of the world. But as this object can only be attained by certain means, it is also necessary to have such means at one's disposal. And what are these means? Faith, hope and love—especially the last.

Here in this adulterous and sinful world, our souls and bodies are continually, and often imperceptibly, corrupted by *moth and rust and thieves*—mental ones— *which break through and steal* the treasures of the soul—*righteousness and peace, and joy in the Holy Ghost.* What is the remedy? The prayer of repentance and of faith. It revives and enlivens our souls corrupted by seductive carnal desires, and drives away the mental thieves; it is a scourge to them, and for us it is the source of power, of life, and of salvation.

It is good for us to live with the prayer of faith in our hearts, for during prayer we live with the Lord, who has promised all good things to those who ask him: *Ask, and it shall be given you; seek, and ye shall find; knock, and it shall be opened. For every one that asketh receiveth; and he that seeketh findeth; and to him that knocketh it shall be opened.*

Unite your soul to God by means of hearty faith, and you will be able to accomplish everything. Do powerful, invisible, ever-watchful enemies wage war against you? You will conquer them. Are these enemies visible, outward? You will conquer them also. Do vices rend you? You will overcome them. Are you crushed with sorrows? You will get over them. Have you fallen into despondency? You will obtain courage. With faith you will be able to conquer everything, and the kingdom of heaven itself will be yours. Faith is the greatest blessing in this earthly life; it unites a man to God, and makes him strong and victorious through him. *He that is joined unto the Lord is one Spirit.*

When you expect to be tempted powerfully by the enemy, arm yourself with all the armour of God, with faith, hope and love. Keep in your heart the words, *All things are possible to him that believeth,* and *Abound in hope, through the power of the Holy Ghost.* Say, 'I do not doubt, I do not despair of, anything good, although you, my enemy, endeavour to sow both doubt and despair in me in regard to everything good, and especially in regard to the highest good, love. The God of love himself is with me, whose children we all are. Unworthy as I am, I bear the image of the Father.'

If you have not enough strength to preserve in your heart the inestimable treasures of faith, hope and love, fall down oftener at the feet of the God of Love. *Ask, and it shall be given you; seek, and ye shall find; knock, and it shall be opened unto you* —for he who has promised is true. Walking, sitting, lying down, conversing or working, at all times pray with your whole heart that faith and love may be given to you. You have not yet asked for them as you should—fervently and constantly with the firm purpose of getting them. Say now. 'I will begin to do so henceforth'.

THREE

The Life of the Spirit

In what does the Christian life consist? In having nothing in the heart but Christ, or, if possessing earthly blessings, in not in the least attaching oneself to them, but in clinging with the whole heart to Christ.

Christ is the Bread of Life; let us therefore lay aside our care about other bread. The God who gives us the Body and Blood of his Son for food and drink will likewise give us our natural bread. He who clothes our soul in Christ will likewise clothe our body. He who condescends to dwell in us will not deprive us of a perishable dwelling.

Our soul is like a heavenly bird, and the Devil like a wicked fowler, seeking to devour souls. As the bird, in flying up to heaven, saves itself from the fowler, so likewise, we, when we see the Devil striving to catch our soul by means of earthly things, must at once forsake these things with all our heart, and must not for a moment attach ourselves to them, but must fly up in our thoughts to Jesus Christ our Saviour, that we may be delivered *from the snare of the fowler*.

Attachment to outward things at once causes coldness towards God and the work of our salvation; coldness towards our neighbour, or hatred and envy towards him, if it depends upon him to give us things, and he does not do so, or if we are obliged to give things to him unwillingly. Therefore it is well to be perfectly indifferent to outward things, in order not to have any occasion for enmity towards our neighbour, which is a great sin. Be above all attachments to this perishable, vain fleeting world; live by your heart in heaven, and love the incorruptible blessings prepared for those who love God and their neighbour.

As we are strangers, sojourners, and travellers to the heavenly kingdom, we must not burden ourselves with worldly cares, nor become attached to earthly blessings, riches, pleasures, honours, lest such cares and attachments hinder us in the hour of death, or make it shameful. The Christian, even here on earth, must accustom himself to live the heavenly life; in fasting, in renunciation, in prayer, love, meekness, gentleness, patience, courage and mercy. How hard will the hour of death be to the man who in his lifetime made his idols of money, or food and drink, or earthly honours! In that hour none of these things shall serve him, while his heart, because it is strongly attached to them, does not possess the true treasure, which would give him life, that is, virtue. And therefore, in order to die more easily—and we must all die—we must not love anything in the world. *And having food and clothing, let us therewith be content.*

That which a man loves, that to which he turns, that he will find. If he loves earthly things, he will find earthly things, and these earthly things will abide in his heart, and will communicate earthiness to him; if he loves heavenly things he will find heavenly things, and they will abide in his heart, and will give him life. We must not set our hearts upon anything earthly, for the spirit of evil is incorporated in all earthly things when we use them immoderately and in excess.

142

All my happiness and unhappiness are in the thoughts and desires of my heart. If the thoughts of my heart are in accord with God's truth, with the will of God, then I am at rest, filled with divine light, joy and blessedness; if not, I am uneasy, filled with spiritual darkness that corrupts the soul, with heaviness and despondency. If I replace the false and ungodly thoughts of my heart by true and godly ones, then rest and blessedness return.

If any thought gives life to the heart, then that thought is true; while, on the contrary, if any thought gives agony and death to the heart, that thought is false. Our Lord is peace and life, and he dwells in our hearts by peace and life.

Peace is the integrity and health of the soul; to lose peace is to lose spiritual health.

When my soul is filled with a holy peace, then surely the King of Peace dwells within me—the Lord Jesus Christ—with the Father and the Holy Ghost; and then above all other times I ought to be full of gratitude to him, and to endeavour with all my strength to preserve this peace within me by means of fervent prayers, and by shunning every sin, whether inward or outward.

The body, as it is only the temporal garment of the soul, is perishable, and its life is not the true life of man. The true life is the spiritual life. If you destroy a man's garment, he himself yet lives; so also after the death and decaying of the body the soul is yet alive. Let us then care principally for the soul, that it may be saved.

Do you pay enough regard to the state of your soul?— whether it is in good health? Whether its life is vigorous? And if its present temporal life is happy, then is its eternal life, its eternal happiness, ensured? Is it ensured, for instance, by faith? Is there in your soul a lively faith in God, in the Lord Jesus Christ, in the Church? Do you practice good works, meekness, humility, gentleness, love of truth and honesty, abstinence, chastity, mercy, patience, obedience, industry, and other such virtues? If you do not, then all your labour is useless. The soul perhaps, does many things worthy of wonder, but it will itself be lost. *For what is a man profited, if he shall gain the whole world, and lose his own soul?*

One must bear in mind that every man possesses, besides his animal nature, a spiritual nature also, and that, as the animal nature has its requirements, the spiritual nature also has its requirements. The requirements of the animal nature are breath, sleep, food, drink, clothing, warmth, light; those of the spiritual nature are meditating, feeling, speaking and communing with God through prayer, divine service, and the sacraments, learning the word of God, and fellowship with our neighbour through mutual converse, assistance and teaching.

We must also bear in mind that our animal nature is temporal, transitory, perishable, whilst the spiritual nature is not transitory, but eternal and indestructible; that we must despise the flesh as perishable, and care for the soul, which is immortal, that it may be saved, enlightened and cleansed from every sin and vice, and adorned with every godly virtue.

The more a man leads the spiritual life, the more spiritual he becomes—he begins to see God in everything, his power and might manifested in everything, and himself always and everywhere abiding in God, and depending upon God even in the smallest matters. But the more a man leads a carnal mode of life, the more carnal he becomes—he sees God in nothing, not even in those things in which his divine power is most wonderfully manifested; everywhere and in everything he sees flesh, matter, and nowhere, nor at any time, is God before his eyes.

He that gathereth not with me scattereth. It is necessary to advance in the spiritual life, to ascend higher and higher, and to increase more and more the stores of our good works. If we stand still at one stage of moral progress, upon one step of the Christian ascent, we fall back; if we do not gather, we scatter.

Often, in matters of ordinary human knowledge, we learn a subject thoroughly once and for all: during the whole of our lifetime our knowledge of it is not obscured. But in matters of faith and religion this is not the case—we think that once we have learnt, felt, and touched it the subject will ever after be clear, tangible, and beloved of our soul; but it is not so. A thousand times it will be obscured from us, removed from us, and as it were vanish away from us, so that at times we feel completely indifferent to that by which we used to live and breathe; and sometimes it will be necessary for us to clear the way to it by sighs and tears, in order to see it clearly once more, to grasp and embrace it with all our heart. This is caused by sin.

FOUR

The Spirit and the Flesh

If the carnal man is at ease and happy, the spiritual man feels oppressed; if the outward man flourishes, the inward man perishes. So opposite in us are the old, sinful, carnal man and the man renewed by Christ's grace; this is why the apostle says, *Though our outward man perish, yet the inward man is renewed day by day.*

The crucified flesh reconciles itself with the spirit and with God; whilst the flesh that is cherished, that is abundantly and daintily fed, fights hard against the spirit and against God, and becomes wholly an abomination of sin. It does not want to pray, and in general rebels against God—for instance, by blasphemy—and estranges itself from him. This is from experience. Therefore, *they that are Christ's have crucified the flesh with the affections and lusts.*

How and when are we to care for the imperishable clothing of the soul, meekness, righteousness, chastity, patience, mercy, and so on, when all our care is directed to perishable clothing and the adornment of our body? We cannot serve two masters, for the soul is simple and single.

How and when are we to care for the spiritual riches of good works, when we long only for perishable riches, and strive to amass wealth with all our means, with all our might, when our heart clings to money and the world, and not to God?

How and when are we to care for the incorruptible food of the spirit, and for the blessed drink—for prayer, the reading of God's word, and the writings and lives of the fathers, and the communion of the Body and Blood of the Lord—when we hardly let food and drink out of our mouths, and this stupefying, nauseating and dangerous smoke which many consider so pleasant?

How can our soul find joy in the Holy Ghost, when we occupy ourselves all the time with earthly and empty pastimes and pleasures? So it is that by serving that which corrupts and destroys we are drawn away from life incorruptible, true and eternal.

The spirit is strong and powerful, and therefore it easily bears a heavy burden; whilst the flesh is inert, and feeble, and is therefore easily overwhelmed by its own natural burden.

The spirit of a man blessed with grace by God's help easily conquers his own flesh, and even the flesh of others; easily masters during prayer the meaning of the words, filling them with his spirit; whilst the carnal man is constantly subjected to his flesh, is oppressed by the words of the prayer, which he is unable to endue with the spirit, or into the pure and holy spirit of which he is unable to penetrate with his own impure and carnal spirit.

So far as a man indulges his sensuality, so far he becomes carnal, and drives away from himself the most Holy Spirit of God, who cannot dwell in those that lead a carnal life. When I gratify my flesh too much, I become my own greatest enemy.

In so far as a man by the grace of God lays aside the carnal life, so far he begins to trample his carnal appetites under foot —he alters his food, ceases to live for his appetite, which he cannot satisfy; gradually faith, hope and love begin to reign in his heart.

IX

THE MORTIFICATION OF THE FLESH

ONE

The Danger of Caring too much for the Flesh

Despise the flesh, for it passeth away.

These hands, that like to take gifts, shall be folded upon the breast, and take no more; these feet, that like to walk for evil, and like not to stand for prayer, shall be stretched out for ever, and shall not go anywhere any more; these eyes, that look with envy upon the prosperity of others, shall close, dimmed for ever, and nothing shall charm them more; the hearing, so often open to listen with pleasure to evil speaking and calumny, shall be no more, and not even thunder will be audible to it: it shall hear only the trumpet arousing the dead, when the incorruptible body shall rise, unto eternal life, or eternal loss. What, then, will live in us, even after our death, and what should be the object of all our care during our present life? That which we now call the heart—that is, the inward man, our soul; this should be the object of our solicitude. Cleanse your heart throughout your life, so that it—or your soul—may be able to see God; only care for your body and its demands so far as is necessary for health, strength and decency. It will all perish; the earth will bear it all away. Strive, therefore, to perfect within you that which loves and hates, that which is calm or disturbed, joyful or sorrowful—your heart, or inward man, which thinks and reasons through your intellect.

It is not enough not to care for pleasures and fine things—do not even care for your own sinful flesh; for by the slightest attachment to all these things you anger God. *While we look not at the things which are seen, but at the things which are not seen; for the things which are seen are temporal, but the things which are not seen are eternal.*

Through our attachment to perishable things we lose sight of the objects which are really natural to our souls, the objects which constitute our true and eternal element; we hew out for ourselves *cisterns, broken cisterns that can hold no water,* and forsake the *Fount of living waters;* we do not turn spiritual, holy, heavenly and lifegiving thoughts into our life, into our blood, but continue to live by worldly, earthly, sinful thoughts and desires, which only oppress, torment, and slay us.

The carnal way of life constitutes death. If you wish to live long, live through the spirit; for life consists in the spirit: *If ye through the spirit do mortify the deeds of the body, ye shall live,* both here on earth and there in heaven. Observe temperance and simplicity in food and drink; preserve chastity; do not foolishly squander the balsam of your life; do not seek after riches or luxury; strive to be contented with little; keep peace with all, respect and love all, envy none; and, above all, strive ever to bear Christ in your heart, and you shall live in peace and felicity for many years.

It is remarkable that, however much we trouble about our health, however much care we take of ourselves, whatever wholesome and pleasant food and drink we take, however much we walk in the fresh air, still, notwithstanding all this, in the end we sicken and corrupt; whilst the saints, who despise the flesh, and mortify it by continual abstinence and fasting, by lying on the bare earth, by watchfulness, labours, unceasing prayer, make both their souls and bodies immortal. Our well-fed bodies decay and after death emit an offensive odour, whilst theirs remain fragrant and flourishing both in life and after death. It is a remarkable thing: we, by building up our body, destroy it, whilst they, by destroying theirs, build it up—by caring only for the fragrance of their souls before God, they obtain fragrance of the body also.

Health and the stomach, these are the idols—particularly with men of today, of whom I myself, a great sinner, am one—the idols for which we live and which we serve continually, even to the neglect of the duties of our Christian calling, such as the reading of the word of God, which is sweeter than honey; prayer, that sweetest converse with God; and the preaching of the word. To walk a great deal for health, and to incite the appetite, to eat with appetite—such are the objects of many of us. But through our frequent walks, through our fondness for food and drink, we shall find that one thing has been neglected, and another irrevocably missed, and yet others have not even entered into our minds. It is not for health and stomach that you must care; you must strive to love God and your neighbour, for these are the two great commandments. *He that dwelleth in love dwelleth in God, and God in him.*

Do not have any solicitude, even for your health, even for your life; give up all your life to the will of the Lord, saying, *for me to live is Christ, and to die is gain.* For, *he that hateth his life in this world, shall keep it unto life eternal.* Attachment to this temporary life, to one's own health, leads to many breaches of God's commandments, to the indulgence of the flesh, to breaking the fasts, to evading the conscientous fulfilment of duty, to despondency, impatience and irritability.

Do not believe your flesh when it threatens you with weakness during prayer; it lies. As soon as you begin to pray you will find that the flesh will become your obedient slave. Your prayer will enliven it also. Always remember that the flesh is lying.

Do not care overmuch for your flesh; do not cherish it, do not gratify it; and do not strengthen it against the spirit. Otherwise when it is necessary to labour in spirit—for instance, to pray, or to write a spiritual or moral work—you will find that the flesh has overpowered the spirit, and has bound it hand and foot. The flesh overthrows all the impulses of the spirit, and will not let it rise and come to its full power. The spirit will then be the slave of the flesh.

In order to please God perfectly, we must also for his sake be perfectly indifferent to our flesh; for example, when during prayer, notwithstanding our slothfulness and strong desire to sleep, we force ourselves not to surrender to it, then we are indifferent to our flesh. The martyrs and ascetics had this perfect indifference to the flesh.

When it is most difficult to fight the flesh, then is the time to show your firmness, then is the time not to grow weak in the conflict, but to fight as a good soldier of Christ.

TWO

How the Enemy Oppresses Us through the Flesh

We are in the habit of saying, 'Had I not looked, I should not have been tempted', 'Had I not heard, I would not have been distressed', 'Had I not tasted of it, I should not have desired further', and so forth. You see how often we are tempted through our own senses. How many have suffered, and still suffer, because they were not firm, because they looked imprudently or impurely, because they listened with undiscerning ears, because they tasted immoderately! The senses of the sin-loving, greedy flesh, uncontrolled by reason and by God's commandments, have darkened them in mind and heart, deprived them both of peace of heart and of free-will, and made them slaves to the senses. Thus you may see how necessary it is so to guard your heart that no sin may steal in through your outward senses, as through a window, and that the Devil, the author of sin, may not in this way wound or kill you.

As long as we lead a carnal life, and do not whole-heartedly draw near to God, so long will the demons hide themselves within us, concealing themselves under the forms of various vices: greed for food and drink, lust, pride, and arrogant free thought concerning the Church and her teachings; malice, envy, avarice, covetousness and so on, so that we live in accordance with them; but as soon as we begin truly to serve the Lord, and thus provoke and strike the demons nestling in us, then they attack us with infernal malice, and manifold, burning attachments to earthly things, until we drive them out of us by fervent prayer, or by partaking of the Holy Sacrament.

It sometimes happens that those who are possessed with evil spirits are calm until they are brought near something holy, but as soon as they approach such a thing, they are overtaken by an extraordinary power, through which they are repelled by the holy thing, they blaspheme and spit at it, and scream. This is why those possessed with evil spirits scream in church during divine service, or when they approach relics; it is be-

155

cause the demons are then met by the blessed power, which is hateful to them, and stronger than them; and which burns, oppresses and strikes them with righteousness, and drives them out of those in whom they dwell.

Thousands of Satan's deceits, by means of food, dress and money, disclose themselves to our spiritual vision, and yet we still continue to be allured by his enticements as though by something real, useful to us, whilst in fact we are caring for what are neither more nor less than destructive illusions, most pernicious to us both spiritually and bodily.

Most men not only bear Satan's burden willingly in their hearts, but become so accustomed to it that often they do not feel it, and even imperceptibly increase it themselves. Sometimes, however, the evil enemy increases his burden tenfold, and then they become terribly despondent and faint-hearted, they murmur and blaspheme God's name. If, instead of turning to vain and wearying amusements, they turn, happily, to God, then the burden is removed from their heart.

Indulgence of the flesh, hardened lack of feeling for everything spiritual and sacred, is the oppressive work of the enemy, although the carnal man does not consider it as such, because he favours it; but those who desire to live a spiritual life look upon it as oppressive, because it prevents God from entering the heart, to enliven and enlighten it, and renders the soul barren of good deeds.

THREE

Sloth and how to Combat it

One of the most powerful wiles of the Devil is to weaken the heart through sloth, and with it to weaken all the spiritual and bodily powers. At such times faith, hope and love are dried up in the heart; we become faithless, despondent, unfeeling to God and man; the salt has lost its savour.

There is sometimes such hardness in the soul that you do not feel, you do not even notice, your sins. You do not fear death, or the Judge, or the terrible judgment-seat; you do not care a jot about anything spiritual. O cunning, proud, evil flesh! It is not without reason that even the saints complain, 'I am overcome with the slumber of sloth, and the sleep of sin oppresses my heart. Make use, my soul, of the time for repentance; shake off the heavy sleep of sloth, and hasten to watch'.

Sometimes your soul is filled with such terrible sloth and lack of feeling that you completely abandon hope of driving them away. It seems as if bodily sickness would be preferable to sloth of this kind.

Do not work only when you wish to, but work also—indeed, above all—when you do not wish to. Do the same in every ordinary worldly matter, and in even more so with regard to the work of saving your soul—prayer, reading the word of God and other salutary books, attending divine service, undertaking good works, whatever they may be, preaching God's word. Do not obey the slothful, lying and most sinful flesh; it is ever ready to rest, and to lead us to eternal death through temporal peace and enjoyment.

Unfortunate is he who immoderately loves the comforts of life, who has surrounded himself with all possible comforts. He will shun every discomfort, he will become effeminate and impatient; but the life of the Christian is all discomfort, a narrow rough way, a cross, requiring discomforts innumerable and great patience. Therefore, Christian wrestler, do not seek for comforts in your dwelling and surroundings; do not love the comforts of this world, but love Christ the cross-bearer. Endure discomfort, and accustom yourself to it.

Remember that Christ was killed on the cross—and that he left the cross to you. Why then do you desire to live in luxury, in grandeur, in indulgence, in idleness? He suffered dishonour and commanded you not to shun dishonour for his name; but you seek honour. Gaze more often upon the cross, and learn what is incumbent upon you. *And they that are Christ's have crucified the flesh with the affections and lusts.*

We must mortify our body with its many demands, and our vices, through abstinence, labour and prayer; and not rouse it and its demands through luxury, gluttony and sloth.

Whosoever will save his life shall lose it. That is, whosoever wishes to save his old carnal, sinful man, shall lose his life: for the true life consists in crucifying and mortifying the old man, together with his deeds, and putting on *the new man, which is renewed in knowledge after the image of him that created him.* Without the mortification of the old, carnal man, there is no true life or eternal blessedness.

158

The more completely, the more ruthlessly, you mortify the old man, the more perfect will be your renewal and rebirth; the more thorough your cleansing, the more perfect will be your life, and the greater your bliss in the age to come. Mortify yourself, and you will find new life.

Unfortunate is he who loves adornment, and seeks the adornment of his body; he will not strive as he ought for the adornment of his soul with faith, love, meekness, humility, righteousness, patience. Especially unfortunate is he who seeks to be adorned with honours; he will make a shameful idol of himself.

We seek after adornment, and adorn ourselves like idols, while we think but little of inward beauty, and entirely forget the inward temple of our soul.

FOUR

Gluttony and Drunkenness

The enemy assaults the heart principally by means of a full stomach. This is from experience.

Food and drink must only be used for strengthening our powers, not for amusement; and when it is not necessary to eat, we must not do so. Many of us (and I myself the worst), if we do not repent and correct ourselves, will be condemned for having eaten and drunk unseasonably, and thus for having lived, though we have understanding, like the brute beasts that have no understanding, and for thus having darkened our foolish hearts. You have amused yourselves with food and drink, and have often eaten and drunk when there was no need for you to eat and drink: *Woe unto you that are full! for ye shall hunger. Ye have lived in pleasure on the earth, and been wanton; ye have nourished your hearts as in a day of slaughter.*

One cannot eat and drink and smoke continually. One cannot turn human life into constant eating, drinking and smoking, although there *are* men who eat, drink and smoke almost without interruption. The spirit of evil has turned life into smoking, and made the mouth, which ought to be employed in thanking and glorifying the Lord, into a smoking furnace. The less and the lighter the food and drink you take, the lighter and more refined will your spirit become.

How fearful it is to use food and drink for amusement, to eat and drink in excess. A full stomach makes a man lose faith and the fear of God, and makes him unfeeling in prayer and thanksgiving to God. An overfed heart turns away from the Lord, and becomes as hard and unfeeling as a stone. This is why the Lord warns us off gluttony and drunkenness: *And so that day come upon you unawares,* because of the wrath of the Lord upon us for heedlessly and idly spending the time in eating and drinking.

The incorporeal enemy enters the heart of a man through gluttony and drunkenness. This can be felt by anyone who is observant. This is why, with the growth of drunkenness, the tendency to drunkenness increases so horribly—the power of the enemy over the man increases. This is why you notice in drunkards a power involuntarily drawing them to satisfy the inward craving for drink. The enemy dwells in the hearts of these unhappy people. How can the demon of drunkenness be driven out? By prayer and fasting. The enemy enters the hearts of men because they have given themselves up to a carnal mode of life—to gluttony—and because they do not pray. It is but natural, therefore, that he can be driven out from them by the opposite means—prayer and fasting.

By feeding largely, one becomes a carnal man, a man of soulless flesh and no spirit; while by fasting one attracts the Holy Ghost and becomes spiritual. When cotton is not soaked with water it is light, and a small quantity of it flies up in the air; but if it is soaked, it becomes heavy and at once falls to the ground. It is the same with the soul. How important it is to preserve it by means of fasting!

Unfortunate is he who is passionately fond of eating and drinking, he who cares overmuch for the pleasures of the table: for he will find, when he begins to labour for the Lord, that food and drink, if we set our heart upon them, are a heavy burden for the body, that they afflict and destroy the spirit, and that man can really satisfy himself with little—very little—and simple food.

Do not believe in the enemy's enticements for one single moment, when the matter is of food and drink, however plausible they may appear to be.

FIVE

Temperance in Food and Drink

You must attend most strictly to your eating and drinking, for upon food and drink, upon what you take, and how much, your activity—internal and external—very greatly depends: *Take heed to yourselves, lest at any time your hearts be overcharged with gluttony and drunkenness.*

Unreasonable and excessive indulgence in tea and coffee is also drunkenness.

When hungry, do not throw yourself upon food—if you do you will overload your heart and your body. Eat slowly, without avidity, remembering to glorify God, who feeds us, and who, above all else, out of love has given himself to us in food and drink—the incorruptible food and drink, his Body and Blood.

Do not hasten to eat and drink, but rather hasten to perform God's service; and when performing God's service, do not think about food and drink.

Those who go to attend divine service after having eaten heavily voluntarily lay upon themselves an unnecessary and harmful burden; they deaden the heart before prayer, and obstruct the access of holy thoughts and feelings to it.

When during prayer the enemy suggests to you a craving for food, despise this irritant, strengthen your heart more powerfully by prayer, and reply to the tempter in the words of the Lord: *Man shall not live by bread alone, but by every word that proceedeth out of the mouth of God*. Prayer is the best food, fortifying and enlightening both soul and body.

Always pray with a fervent heart; and in order to do so never eat and drink excessively.

Let us consider well what makes us careless about saving our soul, which cost the Son of God so dear; what makes us add one sin to another; what makes us fall continually into opposing God, into a life of vanity. Is it not attachment to earthly things, and above all to earthly delights? What makes our heart gross? What makes us become mere flesh, and not spirit, perverting our moral structure? Is it not attachment to food and drink, and other earthly goods?

If you yourself are free from attachments to material things, and give yourself to prayer and fasting, then even in you the spirit will as it were swallow up the flesh, and you will become spiritual, and behold God the Holy Spirit everywhere in nature; whilst on the contrary, those who are attached to earthly things, especially to food and drink, or to money, become *sensual, having not the Spirit*. And in everything they see only flesh, not beholding the spirit, and even rejecting the spiritual aspect of things.

SIX

Fasting and Abstinence

Fasting and abstinence are necessary for us whilst we crave after sensual gratifications.

It is necessary for a Christian to fast, in order to clear his mind, to rouse and develop his feelings, and to stimulate his will to useful activity. These three human powers we blur and stifle above all by *gluttony and drunkenness, and cares of this life*. Through these we fall away from God, the source of life, and fall into foulness and vanity, perverting and defiling the image of God within us. They fasten us to the earth, and cut off so to say, the wings of the soul.

It is also necessary for a Christian to fast because when the Son of God took our human nature upon him, that human nature was uplifted to the divine plane, and now we hasten towards the kingdom of God, which is *not meat and drink; but righteousness and peace, and joy in the Holy Ghost*.

The Christian has great, spiritual, divine enjoyments. Carnal delights must always be subjected to these higher delights; and when they hinder the latter they must be checked or suppressed. It is not to afflict man that food and drink are at certain times and seasons forbidden him by the Church, not to limit his freedom, as worldly people say; it is done in order to afford him true, lasting and eternal delights; for this reason meat or flesh food, and wine and spirits are forbidden during Lent, in order that the heart of man, who is very dear to God, should cling to God alone, and not to anything perishable, unworthy of him.

As sincere, fervent prayer is connected with abstinence, abstinence and fasting are necessary in order to maintain within ourselves the Christian life—the ardour of faith, hope and love. Nothing so soon extinguishes the spirit of faith within us as intemperance, indulgence, excessive search for amusement, and an irregular life.

To what end do fasting and penitence lead? For what purpose is this trouble taken? They lead to the cleansing of the soul from sins, to peace of heart, to union with God; they fill us with devotion and sonship, and give us boldness before God. There are, indeed, very important reasons for fasting and for confession from the whole heart. There shall be an inestimable reward for conscientious labour.

If you eat and drink greedily, then you will be flesh; if you fast and pray, you will be spirit. *Be not drunk with wine, wherein is excess; but be filled with the Spirit.* Fast and pray, and you shall accomplish great things. The overfed man is incapable of great works. But with simple faith you shall accomplish great things, *for all things are possible to him that believeth.*

Fasting is a good teacher: (1) It soon makes everybody who fasts understand that a man needs very little food and drink, and that in general we are greedy and eat a great deal more than is necessary. (2) Fasting clearly discloses all the sins and defects, all the weaknesses and diseases, of our soul, just as when one begins to clean out muddy, stagnant water the reptiles and dirt that lurk in it are revealed. (3) It shows us the necessity of turning to God with the whole heart, and of seeking his mercy, help and saving grace. (4) Fasting shows us all the craftiness, cunning and malice of the bodiless spirits, whom we have hitherto unwittingly served, and who now malignantly persecute us for having ceased to follow them.

Those who reject fasting forget from what the fall into sin of the first men proceeded—intemperance—and what means to counter sin and the tempter were indicated to us by our Lord, when he himself was tempted in the desert—he fasted forty days and nights. They do not know—or do not wish to know —that a man most frequently falls away from God through intemperance.

Begin to fulfil the commandments relating to small things, and you will come to fulfil the commandments relating to great things; everywhere small things lead to great things. Begin by fulfilling the commandment of fasting on Wednesdays and Fridays, or the tenth commandment relating to evil thoughts and desires, and you will eventually learn to fulfil all the commandments. *He that is faithful in that which is least is faithful also in much.*

Those who reject fasting take away from themselves and from others the arms against their flesh, with its manifold vices, and against the Devil, both of which are especially powerful against us through our intemperance. Therefore they are not soldiers of Christ, for they throw down their arms, and give themselves up willingly as prisoners to their sensual and sin-loving flesh.

X

THE MORTIFICATION OF THE FLESHLY SPIRIT

ONE

Humility

To be humble means to consider ourselves deserving for our sins, to be in every way humbled, insulted, persecuted, even struck; and to be meek means patiently to endure injustice, abuse and so forth, and to pray for our enemies.

A deep feeling of spiritual poverty, sorrow at the existence of evil, thirst after salvation—these are to be found in every straightforward and humble soul.

He who is poor in spirit considers himself the very last, the most sinful of all, and reckons himself worthy of being trampled underfoot by all.

Spiritual poverty consists in esteeming oneself as non-existent, and God alone as existing; in honouring his words above everything in the world, and in not sparing anything to fulfil them, not even one's own life; in considering God's will in everything, both for ourselves and others, entirely renouncing our own will.

The man who is poor in spirit desires and says with his whole heart, *Hallowed be thy name, thy kingdom come, thy will be done, as in heaven, so on earth*. It is as though he himself disappears; everywhere and in everything he wishes to see God—in himself and in others. 'Let everything be thine, not mine'.

He wishes to contemplate God's holiness in himself and in all his kingdom, and likewise his will; also to see him, alone, entirely filling the human heart; as it should be, for he alone is all-merciful, all-perfect, all-creating.

He who is poor in spirit does not dare to try, does not think of trying, to comprehend the incomprehensible, to penetrate God's secrets, to philosophise on the highest; he believes in the word of the Lord, the Life-giver, knowing that his every word is truth, spirit, and life eternal; and in the words of his Church, ever instructed in all truth by the Holy Ghost, he believes as a child believes his father or mother, not demanding proofs, but relying upon them in perfect trust.

To him who is poor in spirit the whole world is as nothing. Everywhere he sees God alone giving life to everything, and ruling everything; for him, there is no place without God, no moment without God; everywhere, and at every minute, he is with God, and as though with him alone.

If you wish to be truly humble, then consider yourself lower than all, worthy of being trampled on by all; for you yourself daily, hourly, trample upon the law of the Lord, and therefore upon the Lord himself.

Welcome everyone who comes to you with a kind and cheerful aspect, although he or she may be a beggar, and humble yourself inwardly before everybody, counting yourself lower than all, for you are called by Christ himself to be the servant of all, and all are his members, although—like you—they bear the wounds of sin.

To be gentle, humble and kind to all, even to our enemies, to be simple, disinterested, contented with little, the little that is indispensable, to be generous and full of good-will to everyone—such are the things that unite us to God, the source of life, and to other men by endearing us to them.

You *must* be humble, meek and long-suffering; remembering that you are clay, dust, nothing; that you are impure; that everything good that you have is of God; that your life, your breath, and everything you possess are God's gifts; that for your sins you ought now to redeem your future blessedness in Paradise by the long-suffering which is indispensable in this imperfect and sin-ridden world.

If you truly wish to be humble, then long to be in every way offended and persecuted, as a hungry man longs for food; for by the justice of God you are worthy of this.

When you are disturbed and sick at heart because you are slandered, it shows that pride is in you, and that it must be wounded and expelled by outward dishonour. Therefore do not be irritated by scorn, and do not bear malice towards those who hate and slander you, but love them as your physicians, whom God has sent to instruct you and to teach you humility, and to pray to God for them. Thank God for outward dishonour; those who endure dishonour here will not be subjected to it in the next world. *She hath received of the Lord's hand double for all her sins. Lord, thou wilt ordain peace for us: for thou also hast wrought all our works in us.*

If you meet with disregard, or even contempt, from strangers, do not be hurt, or take offence at it, but say to yourself, I deserve this. Glory to thee, O Lord, that thou hast granted unto me, who am unworthy, to receive dishonour from men like unto myself.

When anyone out of kindness praises you to others, and they pass on these praises to you, do not consider them as a just tribute of esteem really due to you, but ascribe them solely to the kindness of heart of the person who spoke of you in this way, and pray for him that God may strengthen him in his kindness of heart and in every virtue; but acknowledge yourself to be the greatest of sinners, not just out of humility, but truthfully, actually, knowing as you do your evil deeds.

Should thoughts of self-praise, of self-satisfaction, occur to you, remind yourself that you are nothing, and that all that is good in you is accomplished by the grace of God. *What has thou that thou didst not receive? Without me ye can do nothing.* Should the thought of despising any of your neighbours, or of your family, come to you, remind yourself that man is the work of God's hands, and that *it was very good.*

TWO

Pride

There is absolutely nothing for a Christian to be proud of in accomplishing works of righteousness, for he is saved, constantly delivered, from every evil through faith alone; in the same manner he accomplishes works of righteousness also by the same faith. *For by grace are ye saved through faith; and that not of yourselves; it is the gift of God, not of works, lest any man should boast.*

When the foolish thought of counting up any of your good works enters your head, at once correct your fault, and instead count up your sins, your repeated and numberless offences, and you will find that they are as the sand of the sea, whilst your virtues in comparison are as nothing.

When we hear anything bad of anyone, then, inwardly comparing him with ourselves, we say in our heart, 'I am not like that; I am perfect compared to him'; and thinking thus of ourselves, and inwardly judging others, we are delighted that we are so much better than they. This is the pride of Satan; this is the stench of the carnal, sinful man. May such thoughts flee from the soul! Let us consider ourselves as the worst of all men. When we hear anything bad of anyone, let us say to ourselves, 'We are worse, a hundred times worse, than this man', and let us pray from our whole soul for the convicted brother.

Pride shows itself particularly in the fact that the man who is infected with it makes himself equal to all, or at any rate to many, who surpass him in age, strength, and ability, and cannot bear to be considered beneath them. If a proud man is a subordinate, he does not respect his superior as he ought, does not like to greet him properly, and does not respect his orders, but fulfils them unwillingly, and only out of fear. He makes himself equal to better educated people, and does not acknowledge anyone to be superior to himself, or else acknowledges the superiority of only very few indeed. If he is a learned—or even an unlearned—son, he does not pay due respect to his parents and benefactors, particularly those who are simple and rough folk, considering himself equal to, or even above them.

Our self-love and pride manifest themselves especially in impatience and irritability, when some of us cannot bear the slightest unpleasantness . caused us by others, whether intentionally or unintentionally, or any obstacle, lawful or not, deliberate or not, put in our path.

Our self-love and pride would like everything to be as we wish, that we should be surrounded by every honour and comfort in this temporal life; would like all men, and even—so far do we carry our pride—all nature itself, speedily and silently to obey us; while we ourselves are very slow in faith and in every good work—slow to please the one master of all.

In order to rule others, we must first learn to rule ourselves; in order to teach others, we must acquire knowledge ourselves. If I do not know how to control myself, if I have no spirit of self-command, the spirit of meekness, holiness, love and righteousness, then I shall direct others badly. If I am the sport of every kind of vice, it is better for me not to undertake to rule others, lest I do greater harm than good, both to myself and to them.

You must take the utmost care not to compare yourself with others in any respect, but always to put yourself below others, although in fact you *may* be equal to, or even better than, others in some respects.

Everything that is good in us is the free gift of God; nothing is our own. *And that not of yourselves: it is the gift of God: not of works, lest any man should boast.* And how can we take pride in a goodness that is not ours, and make ourselves equal to those whom God has placed higher than us?

THREE

The Acceptance of Reproof

We are often angry with frank and outspoken people for dis-closing our faults. We ought on the contrary not merely to forgive such people, but to value them, if by bold speaking they break down our self-love. They are moral surgeons who with a sharp word cut out the rottenness of the heart, and they awaken, in the soul deadened by sin, a consciousness of sin, and a quickening reaction.

Sometimes people teach you by means of hints which you can-not endure, and you are vexed with your teachers. We must endure and listen with love to everything useful coming from any one, whoever he may be. Our self-love conceals our faults from us, but they are more visible to others. This is why they remark upon them. Bear in mind that *we are members one of another,* and are therefore obliged even to correct one another. If you cannot bear others to teach you, and are vexed with them for doing so, it means that you are proud, and shows clearly that the fault at which others hint really is in you, and needs to be corrected.

Value highly, and always preserve, Christian meekness and kindness, mutual peace and love, crushing by every possible means the impulses of self-love, malice, irritability, and dis-turbance. Do not be angered, do not even be disturbed, when anybody tells you a falsehood to your face, or makes any unjust pretension, or speaks offensively, or boldly detects any of your weaknesses or vices, the wrongfulness of which, through your self-love, you did not suspect.

Always first coolly reflect upon what your opponent says, as well as upon your own words and conduct, and if, upon an entirely impartial consideration of your words and actions, you find them just, then let your conscience be at rest, and take no notice of the words of your adversary, either remaining silent, or showing him his error quietly and gently, in all kindness of heart.

Should you find yourself guilty of that which some other person detects in you, then, putting aside self-love and pride, ask pardon for your fault, and endeavour to correct yourself in the future.

When others reproach us with anything, it should not irritate us, nor make us despondent; rather it should humble us, who are morally worthless, and should make us turn to God with the fervent prayer that he may heal our sicknesses, and by his grace supply that which is wanting in us.

To grow irritated when reproached, and above all when we are reproached with faults which we really do possess, would only be adding one malady to another, one vice to another; it would mean that we are sick with the wilful blindness of self-love, which does not wish to see its own dark side, and leads us to destroy ourselves of our own will.

To despond when reproached is also most foolish, for by the help of God's grace the Christian can always change for the better if he wishes to do so; and it is for this purpose that the Lord sends us accusers, that we may open our spiritual eyes,

176

and see the deformity of our deeds, and so correct ourselves; it is not that we may cast ourselves into despondency. Despondency is itself a sin, and the work of the Devil.

Reproof ought to produce in us the *godly sorrow, which worketh repentance to salvation,* and not the sorrow of self-love.

FOUR

Irritability

The Christian has no reason to harbour in his heart any ill-feeling whatever towards any one. Such ill-feeling, like every other evil, is the work of the Devil. The Christian must have only love in his heart; and as love cannot think evil, he cannot have any ill-feeling towards others.

He who is impatient and irritable does not know himself and the human race, and is unworthy of the name of Christian. In saying this I pronounce judgment against myself, for I am the first of those who are afflicted with impatience and irritability.

Irritability of temper proceeds from lack of self-knowledge, from pride, and also from the fact that we do not consider how greatly corrupted is our nature, and know but little the meek and humble Jesus.

Our self-love and pride manifest themselves especially in impatience and irritability, when some of us cannot bear the slightest unpleasantness caused us by others, whether intentionally or unintentionally, or any obstacle, lawful or not, deliberate or not, put in our path.

Keep a strict watch against every appearance of pride; it appears imperceptibly, particularly when you are vexed or irritable with others for unimportant reasons.

We ought not to allow ourselves to be vexed or irritated by anything, because if we do become vexed or irritated frequently we form a habit which is very harmful to us, both morally and physically, whilst if we bear opposition with equanimity we form a good and beneficial habit—that of enduring everything calmly and patiently.

Many occasions for vexation may arise in this life through our innumerable mutual imperfections, and if we were to become irritated upon every such occasion we would not live more than a few months.

FIVE

Malice

God is glorified by nothing so much as by the *charity that beareth all things,* and is dishonoured and offended by nothing so much as by malice, under whatever fair appearance it may hide itself.

Fear malice as you fear the fire; do not admit it into your heart, no matter how plausible the pretence—still less on account of anything offensive to yourself; malice is always an evil, a child of hell.

Unfortunately the Devil shelters himself behind us, and conceals himself while we are blind, and thinking we act of ourselves begin to stand up for the Devil's works, as if they were our own, as if for something just, although every idea of there being any justice in the vice of malice is entirely false and harmful.

When you see that anyone bears malice towards you, do not consider his malice as his own; he is only the passive instrument of the evil one, whose flattery he has not yet recognised. Pray to God that the enemy may leave him, and that the Lord may enlighten the eyes of his heart, darkened by the foul breathing of the spirit of evil.

When malice against any one is roused in your heart, then believe firmly that it is the work of the Devil; hate him and his brood, and malice will leave you. Do not acknowledge it as anything of your own, and do not sympathise with it. This is from experience.

Do not let the Devil sow enmity and malice in your heart; do not let these feelings nestle there in any way; if you do, your malice, even if not expressed in words, but shown only in your glance, may infect the soul of your brother also, for nothing is as infectious as malice; above all it easily infects those who have an abundance of it stored away in the heart, and fans the spark of evil in them into a flame.

If anyone has offended you, do not bear malice, and when he who has offended you looks kindly upon you and turns to speak to you, do not let your heart incline to evil, but talk pleasantly and good-humouredly to him, as if nothing had happened between you; learn to conquer evil by good, malice by kindness, meekness and humility.

How incessantly the hater of mankind offers us one pretext after another for hating our neighbour, so that we are almost constantly angry with others, almost constantly bearing malice, and living in accordance with his infernal all-destroying will. Do not let us run after his phantoms; let us put aside all enmity, and love everyone, for love is of God.

Sometimes malice enters the heart under the pretence of zeal for the glory of God or the good of our neighbour. Do not believe in your zeal in such a case; it is false and unwise; rather be zealous that there should not be any malice in you.

Do not give way to the dark evil feelings in your heart, but conquer and uproot them by the power of faith, and by the light of a sound mind, and you will become kind and gentle. Such feelings frequently arise in the depths of the heart. He who has not learned to subdue them will often be gloomy and melancholy, a burden to himself and to others. When they come to you, force yourself to be cheerful and pleasant, to mirth and innocent jests, and they will be dispersed like smoke. This is from experience.

XI

THE SPIRITUAL LIFE IN THE WORLD

ONE

The Love of God and our Neighbour

The purer the heart becomes, the larger it becomes; consequently it is able to find room for more and more loved ones; the more sinful it is, the more it contracts; consequently it is able to find room for fewer and fewer loved ones—it is limited by a false love: self-love.

To love God with all our heart means not to have any attachments to anything earthly, and to surrender the whole heart to the Lord God, fulfilling his will, and not our own, in all things. To love God with all the soul means always to have all our mind in him, to establish all our heart in him, and to submit all our will to his will in every circumstance of life, both joyful and sorrowful; to love God with all our strength means to love him in such a way that no opposing power, nor any circumstance of life, shall be able to separate us from the love of God; to love God with all our understanding means always to think of God, of his mercy, long-suffering, holiness, wisdom, might, and of his works, and to withdraw ourselves by every means from thoughts of vanity and evil. To love God means to love righteousness with all our soul, and to hate wickedness, as it is written: *Thou hast loved righteousness and hated iniquity;* to love God means to hate oneself—that is, to hate our old, carnal man: *If any man come to me, and hate not his own life, he cannot be my disciple.* To love God means to fulfil his commandments: *If a man love me, he will keep my words. He that loveth me not, keepeth not my sayings.*

How can we love God with all our heart, with all our soul, and all our strength, and all our thoughts? With all our heart means undividedly, not sharing our love between God and the world, or between God and creatures. If, for instance, you pray, pray with an undivided heart, not allowing yourself to be distracted; be wholly *in* God, in his love, with all your soul —that is, do not love him with only part of your soul; not only with your mind, without your heart and will sharing in your love; with all your strength, not with half your strength, or slightly. When you have to fulfil any commandment, fulfil it with zeal, unto sweat and blood, unto laying down your life for it, if necessary, and not slothfully, indolently and unwillingly.

Love for God begins to manifest itself, and to act in us, when we begin to love our neighbour as ourselves, and not to spare ourselves or anything belonging to us for him, as he is the image of God: *For he that loveth not his brother, whom he hath seen, how can he love God, whom he hath not seen?*

We stand before the altar of love, before the very presence of Love Incarnate himself; and we have no love for each other! Is it not strange? And worse, we do not even worry about it, do not care about it. But love will not come of itself—we must strive for it with earnest efforts.

We are accustomed to the works of God, and therefore value them but little; we do not, for instance, value even man as we ought to—man, the greatest work and miracle of God's omnipotence and grace. Look upon every man, whether he is one of your family, or a stranger to you, as upon something perpetually new in God's world, as upon God's greatest miracle; do not let the fact of your being accustomed to him serve as a reason for neglect. Esteem and love every man as your own self, constantly, unchangeably.

He who is insolent towards man is insolent towards God, as many of us are. Respect in man the grand, inestimable image of God, and be forbearing towards the faults and errors of fallen men, so that God may be forbearing towards yours; for the enemy of God and of mankind, unable to vent his malice upon God, endeavours to vent it upon his image, man.

It is necessary that the following words should be engraved indelibly upon our hearts: *Thou shalt love thy neighbour as thyself.* These words must guide our heart upon meeting with any one, at any time, whether he comes to us, or we go to him; whether we have to do some work for him, or to give him anything, or simply to converse with him. Bear in your heart the words *love him as thyself,* and carry on a perpetual war with yourself for the observance of these living words of our Lord. Force yourself to love.

Love every man as yourself—that is, do not wish him anything that you do not wish for yourself; think, feel, for him, just as you would think and feel for your own self; do not wish to see in him anything that you do not wish to see in yourself; do not let your memory cherish any evil done to you by others, just as you would wish that the evil done by yourself should be forgotten by others; do not deliberately imagine in yourself or in others anything wicked or impure; believe others to be as well-disposed as yourself, unless you see clearly that they are ill-disposed; do unto them as you would to yourself, and not otherwise, and you will find in your heart great peace and blessedness. *He that dwelleth in love dwelleth in God and God in him.*

To love your neighbour as yourself, to sympathise with him in his joy and his sorrow, to feed, to clothe him, if he is in need of food and clothing; to breathe, so to say, the same air with him—look upon all this as the same thing as feeding and warming yourself, and do not count these as virtues or as works of love to your neighbour, lest you grow proud of them. *For we are members one of another.*

In order to find out whether you love your neighbour in accordance with the gospel, take note of yourself when others offend you, abuse you, mock you, or do not render you the respect due to you, or which is customary, or when your subordinates err and are negligent. If you remain calm on such occasions, are not filled with a spirit of enmity, hatred, impatience; if you continue to love these persons as much as previously, then you do love your neighbour in accordance with the gospel; but if you become irritable, angry, agitated, then you do not. *If ye salute your brethren only, what do ye more than others?*

God is long-suffering and merciful to you; this you experience many times every day. Be long-suffering and merciful to your brethren, then, fulfilling the words of the apostle, who thus speaks of charity before all else: *Charity suffereth long and is kind.* You desire that the Lord should gladden you by his love; for your part gladden the hearts of others by your love, tenderness and kindness.

Rejoice at every opportunity of showing kindness to your neighbour as a true Christian who strives to store up as many good works as possible, especially the treasures of love.

Do not rejoice when others show you kindness and love, but consider yourself unworthy of it; rejoice, on the other hand, when an occasion presents itself for you to show love to others. Show love simply, without straying into cunning thoughts, without calculating in a petty, worldly and covetous way, remembering that love is God himself. Remember that he sees all your ways, all the thoughts and movements of your heart.

Love your neighbour as yourself; for by loving your neighbour you love yourself, whilst by hating your neighbour you harm your own soul above all else, you hate your own soul before all else.

Do not despise any man, no matter who or what he be; but behave respectfully and kindly to every man of good will, above all to the poor, as to our members worthy of sympathy, mercy and pity; otherwise you will wound your own soul cruelly.

Contempt for the creature touches the Creator; therefore never dare to speak words such as 'I dislike that man's face, though he may be a good man', for this is a devilish hatred for God's creature. Remember, that every man is an image of God, and that all his glory is within him, in his heart. Man looks upon the face; God looks upon the heart.

Christ the Son of God *is not ashamed to call us sinners brethren;* therefore be not ashamed to call poor, obscure, simple people your brethren, whether they be your relatives according to the flesh or not; do not behave proudly towards them, do not despise them, for we are all brothers in Christ—all born of water and the Spirit in the baptismal font, all therefore the children of God, all nourished with the Body and Blood of the

Son of God; the sacraments of the Church are celebrated over all of us, we all pray the Lord's Prayer.

If I despise or hate anybody, it shows that I unlawfully exalt and love myself—that is, my flesh. Our heart continually flatters us, secretly exalting ourselves, secretly lowering others. But we must constantly see our numberless sins, in order to judge ourselves, to weep over ourselves, as for the spiritually dead. Then we shall not have time to notice the faults of others, and to condemn our neighbours for them, or to despise them; but we shall esteem them, for we shall find that they are incomparably better than us in many things.

Love every man in spite of his falling into sin. Never mind the sins, remember that the man is still the image of God. Other people's weaknesses strike us, but we too are not without evil—perhaps, even, there is more in us than in others. At least in respect to sin men are equal: *For all have sinned and come short of the glory of God*. Therefore, besides loving each other, we must bear with each other, and pardon each other, in order that we also may be forgiven. Therefore, with all your soul honour and love in every man the image of God, not regarding his sins, for God alone is holy, God alone is without sin; and see how much he loves us, how much he has created and still creates for us, punishing us mercifully and forgiving us so abundantly. Honour the man also, in spite of his sins, because he can always amend.

The love of God is so great, so immeasurable, that beside it all human dislike, enmity and hatred become insignificant, and seem to vanish entirely. It is because God's love for us is boundless, and human enmity so insignificant that the Lord commanded us all to love our enemies, to bless them that curse us, to do good to them that use us despitefully and persecute us. We abide in the love of God; does it greatly matter if men are not well-disposed towards us? What can they do against us when God has so loved us?

We are darkened by our own vices, and do not see the monstrous folly of our conduct, but when the Lord enlightens us by the light of his grace, then, as if awaking from sleep, we see clearly this monstrous folly of our feelings, thoughts, words and deeds; our heart, which until then was hardened, softens; the evil passes away, and is replaced by mercy, kindness and generosity. Therefore we must also love our enemies, as it is written: *Love your enemies, bless them that curse you, and pray for them which despitefully use you, and persecute you—* for they, our brethren, are also blind, have also gone astray.

TWO

Our Attitude to the Sins of Others

Do not confound man, the image of God, with the wickedness that is in him, for the wickedness is only accidental, his misfortune, a sickness, an illusion of the Devil; but his being, the image of God, still remains.

Sinners, esteem one another, and do not despise any sinner, for we are all sinners, and the Son of God came to save, to cleanse, and to raise us all up to heaven.

Do not observe the sins of others, and do not behave with enmity, inward or outward, towards those who sin; but represent to yourself your own sins, and repent heartily of having committed them, considering yourself in reality worse than all. Pray lovingly for those who sin, knowing that we are all inclined to every sin.

When your brother sins against you in any way, do not be angry with him, but seek to find in him those good qualities which undoubtedly exist in every man, and dwell lovingly on them, despising his offences against you as dross not worth attention, as an illusion of the Devil.

What would it be like if every one of us were to notice all his neighbour's offences? Eternal animosity and discord; for who is without sin? Therefore we are commanded to forgive all those that trespass against us; for if the Lord will be extreme to mark our sins, which of us may abide his justice? *For if ye forgive men their trespasses, your heavenly Father will also forgive you.*

The Lord taught us to look indulgently upon the frequent falls of men, and to say, *Forgive us our debts, as we forgive our debtors. All things whatsoever ye would that men should do unto you, do ye even so unto them.* And which of us does not wish that others should be indulgent and long-suffering with him?

You easily forgive yourself if you have sinned; forgive other people as easily. By this love is known. Even this is little for love to do; love loves its enemy, does good to them which hate it, blesses them that curse it, and prays for them which despitefully use it.

You are angry with your neighbour, and say of him that he has done this or that, and so on. What business of yours is it? He sins against God, not against you. God is his judge, not you, and to God he shall give an account of himself, not to you. Know how sinful you are yourself, how difficult it is for you to master your own sins, and to get the better of them, how afflicted you are by them, how they have ensnared you, how you wish indulgence from others. Your brother is a man like unto you; therefore you must be indulgent to him, as to a sinful man similar in all things to you, as infirm as you. Love him, then, as yourself: *These things I command you, that ye love one another.*

You hate your enemy? You are foolish. Why? Because if the enemy persecutes you, you also inwardly persecute yourself most cruelly when you say that you hate your enemy, when you torture yourself by your hatred of him. Love your enemy; that is wise.

A man who is wrathful is a sick man; we must cure him by applying love to his heart. We must treat him kindly, speak to him gently. And if there is no deep-rooted malice in him, but only a temporary fit of anger, you will see how his heart will melt through your kindness and love. You will see how good will conquer evil.

Do not let yourself be angered by anything. Remember that as you are infirm, so is your neighbour, and that one infirmity is cancelled by another. It is useless to blame the infirm and sinful, if they acknowledge their infirmity; we must blame the Devil, who is so powerful in evil.

He who does any evil, who gratifies any passion, is punished enough by the evil he has committed, by the vice he has served, and above all by the fact that he withdraws himself from God, and God withdraws himself from him—it would therefore be insane, and inhuman, to nourish anger against such a man; one might as well drown a man who is already sinking, or push into the fire one who is already burning. To such a man, as to one in danger of perishing, we must show more love than ever, and pray fervently for him, not judging him, nor rejoicing at his misfortune.

Matters cannot be set right by vexation and irritation, but, on the contrary, only become worse. Therefore, it is better always to keep calm, even always to show love and respect for morally sick humanity, or, to speak more particularly, for our relatives, friends and subordinates. For man is not an angel, and our life is so constituted that we sin every day, and almost involuntarily—even though we do not wish to do so: *For the good that I would, I do not; but the evil, which I would not, that I do.*

When reprimanding the faults of your subordinates, take care not to give way to anger, not to be irritated or overwrought; be gentle, loving and calm, and preserve your dignity. If the subordinate you have to correct takes offence, gently observe to him that you do not intend to irritate or offend him, that you sincerely wish him well, and that he should be orderly in his work; make it clear that it is not him that you are annoyed with, but the disorder which he causes. Do not offend his pride and dignity by exalting yourself in his eyes and lowering him. If you have this weakness of pride, you had better leave correcting others to someone else, and first cure yourself: *First cast the beam out of thine own eye; and then thou shalt see clearly to cast the mote out of thy brother's eye.* Otherwise you will only succeed in irritating your brother, and you will not do him any moral good.

You are angry with your neighbour, you despise him, you do not like to speak peaceably and lovingly to him, for some reason or other? But you yourself are worse than he is. *Physician, heal thyself.* Teacher, teach thyself. Your own malice is the bitterest of all evils. Is it then possible to correct malice by malice, evil by evil? Having a plank in your own eye, can you pull out the splinter from the eye of another?

Evil is corrected by good; faults by love, kindness, meekness, humility and patience. Acknowledge yourself as the greatest of sinners, of those who appear to you to be sinners, or are sinners in fact; consider yourself worse and lower than all; wrest out all pride and malice against your neighbour, all impatience and bad temper, and only then try to cure others. Until then, cover the sins of others with your indulgent love.

If you are angry with your brother on account of his sins, even supposing that they *are* particularly offensive, then re-collect that you yourself are not without offensive sins, although they may be different ones. You desire that your shameful sins should be covered by the indulgence of others; recollect how thankful you would be to them, how you would embrace them for such enduring love, how such indulgence would lighten your already heavy sorrow for your sins, and would strengthen your weakness in struggling with them, would strengthen your spirit by suggesting trust in God's mercy. Then you must desire the same indulgence for your brother, who is your member and a member of Christ. *Thou shalt love thy neighbour as thyself.* And if you wish your sins to be forgiven you, you must forgive your brother's sins against you: *For if ye forgive men their trespasses, your heavenly Father will forgive you: but if ye forgive not men their trespasses, neither will your Father forgive your trespasses.*

Do not be offended if any one speaks or behaves insincerely to you; do you yourself always speak and behave sincerely? Are you not often hypocritical? Do you always pray sincerely, and not hypocritically? Do not your lips often speak the truth, while your heart is lying? Do you always walk before God in sincerity and simplicity? If you yourself are not right before God and men, if you are often false, often hypocritical, then do not be angry if others are false and hypocritical with you. *Wherewithal a man sinneth, by the same also shall he be punished.* Be indulgent to others who sin in the same way as you do.

Do not be irritated with those who sin; do not develop a habit of noticing every sin in others, and of judging them, as we are so inclined to do. Everyone shall give an answer to God for himself. Correct your *own* sins; and amend your *own* heart.

Bear always in mind the words of the Lord's Prayer: *And forgive us our trespasses, as we forgive them that trespass against us.* These words should always remind us that we ourselves at all times are great trespassers, great sinners before God, and that, mindful of this, we should be humble in the depths of our hearts, and not be very sincere to the faults of our brethren, who are weak like ourselves; that as we do not judge ourselves severely, we must not judge others severely, for our brethren are our own members.

Charity thinketh no evil. To think evil is the work of the Devil: it is the Devil in the man who makes him think evil. Therefore do not bear any ill-feeling in your heart towards another, and do not think evil lest you become united to the Devil. The evil which you see or suspect overcome with good.

194

I must not think that anyone else is evil or proud unless I have positive reasons for thinking so.

It is better not to pass on words of reproach which we have heard; rather we should keep silence concerning them, or pass on words of love and good will. Then we shall be calm in spirit. But to pass on words of animosity and envy is very hurtful; they often produce—in the impatient and self-loving men to whom they refer—a spiritual tempest; they rekindle extinct enmity, they occasion dissension. We must have Christian patience, and the wisdom of the serpent.

Attend not to the actual words of an arrogant man, but rather to his meaning. It often happens that words which appear harsh at first do not in fact proceed from any harshness of heart, but only from habit. How would it be if everyone examined *our* words strictly and critically, without Christian love—indulgent, kindly, long-suffering?

Sometimes the enemy cunningly attacks us in such a way that when we see any sin or vice in our brother, or in the community, our heart is stricken with indifference, coldness and reluctance—or rather, shameful cowardice—to utter a firm reproach.

Charity, it is said, *rejoiceth not in iniquity, but rejoiceth in the truth*. We often see the unrighteous and sinful deeds of men, or hear of them, and we have a sinful habit of rejoicing at such deeds, and of shamelessly expressing this joy by foolish laughter. This is wrong, unchristian, uncharitable, impious. It shows that we have not Christian love for our neighbour in our hearts. Let us therefore break with this habit, that we may not be condemned with the workers of iniquity.

THREE

Good Works

We must remember that it is impossible to do good works without effort. Since our voluntary falling into sin the kingdom of God cannot be taken otherwise than by *violence, and the violent take it by force.*

Seek ye first the kingdom of God, and his righteousness; and all these things shall be added unto you. How are we to seek first the kingdom of God? In the following manner: let us suppose that you wish to go somewhere on any temporal business; before doing so, first pray to the Lord that he may correct the ways of your heart, and then also the present way of your body, or that he may direct the way of your life in accordance with his commandments; desire this with all your heart, and often renew this prayer. The Lord, noting your sincere desire and endeavour to walk in accordance with his commandments, will, by degrees, correct all your ways.

The way to succeed in any good work. When you pray, at home, in the morning or the evening, or in church, during divine service, be solicitous in your heart to accomplish this particular good work, and desire whole-heartedly to fulfil it to the glory of God. The Lord and his immaculate Mother will teach you how to accomplish it.

In all that you do, at home and at your work, do not forget that all your strength, all your success, all your light, are in Christ and his cross; therefore, be sure to call upon the Lord before beginning any work, saying, Jesu, help me! Jesu enlighten me! So will your heart be supported and warmed by lively faith and hope in Christ, for his is *the power and the glory unto the ages of ages.*

If you love your neighbour, then all heaven will love you; if you are united in spirit with your fellow-creatures, then you will be united with God and all the company of heaven; if you are merciful to your neighbour, then God and all the angels and saints will be merciful to you; if you pray for others then all heaven will intercede for you. The Lord our God is holy; be holy yourself also.

Deny yourself sensual delights in the hope that, instead of them, you will get higher, spiritual, heavenly delights. Do good to all in the hope that, in accordance with the justice of God, *with what measure ye mete, it shall be measured to you in return;* that the good you have done to your neighbour shall sooner or later be returned into your bosom, just as the evil you have done him shall sooner or later be returned into your bosom. Remember that we are one body. Remember that God is absolutely just.

197

FOUR

Almsgiving

What is false gratitude to God? Gratitude is false when, having received bountiful, undeserved spiritual and material gifts from God, people thank God for them with their tongue, and use them only for their own advantage, not sharing them with their neighbours; when they obtain them and conceal them in their banks or galleries or libraries, or what have you, and thus deprive many of their brethren of enlightenment, of instruction, and of consolation; or of food, drink, clothing or dwelling; or of healing; or of the means of moving in order to get a living. Such gratitude is false and ungodly. It is thanking God with the tongue, and at the same time showing extreme ingratitude in deed. But how many such 'grateful' men there are!

Thou shalt love thy neighbour as thyself. We ought to have all things in common. As the sun, the air, fire, water and earth are common to us all, so also ought food and drink, money, books, and, in general, all the Lord's gifts to be shared in common, at any rate to some extent; for they are given in common to all, and yet may easily be divided and distributed amongst many. We have nothing of our own; everything belongs to God.

When I look more closely upon some of the poor, and talk with them, then I see how meek, lovable, humble, simple-hearted, truly kind, poor in body, but rich in spirit they are. They make me—who am harsh, proud, evil, scornful, irritable, crafty, cold towards God and men, full of envy and avarice—ashamed of myself. These are the true friends of God. And the enemy, being aware of their spiritual treasures, awakens in his servants—the proud and rich—contempt and ill-feeling towards them, and would like to wipe them off the face of the earth, as if they had no right to live and walk upon it.

Friends of my God, my poor brethren! It is you who are the truly rich in spirit, whilst I am the real beggar, accursed and poor. You are worthy of sincere respect from us, who possess the blessings of this world in abundance, but who are poor and needy in virtues, and in love towards God and our neighbour. May the Lord teach us to despise outward things, and to look upon the inward, to value the inward and not the outward, and to observe this in our dealings with the rich and powerful of this world.

It is not just for the rich to keep excess wealth when there are many poor people in need of the means of existence, of necessary clothing and dwellings. The crying poverty arising from old age, exhaustion, sickness, fruitless or badly paid labour, really difficult conditions of life, a numerous family, bad harvests; this we must always hasten to help, especially those of us who are rich.

God did not spare for our sakes even his only-begotten Son. How, then, after this can we grudge anything to our neighbour —food, drink, clothing, or money for his needs? The Lord gives much to some, and little to others in order that we may provide for one another. The Lord has so ordered that if we willingly share the bountiful gifts of his mercy with others, then they serve to benefit us by opening our hearts to the love of our neighbour, while our moderate use of them serves to benefit our body, which does not become overloaded by them.

Watch yourself when a poor man, who is in need of your help, asks it of you. The enemy will endeavour at that time to chill your heart, and fill it with indifference and even scorn, towards him that is in want. Overcome this; incite your heart to love of this man like unto you all in all respects, to this member of Christ, your own member, in order that Christ the Lord may love and help you too; and, whatever the needy may ask of you, fulfil his request according to your power. *Give to him that asketh thee, and from him that would borrow of thee turn thou not away.*

When you give alms to one who begs of you, and who, apparently, does not deserve it, or does not need it, owing to which your heart grudges him the alms given, repent of this; for the God of Love continues to bestow his blessings upon us, even when we have enough already. Love for your neighbour ought to say to you, 'Even though he has something, still it will do no harm if I add to his prosperity (although in fact a few pence will not greatly increase or amend his fortunes). God gives to me, why then should I not give to the needy?' I say, to the needy, for who would hold out his hand without need? Had God only bestowed gifts upon you in accordance with your merits, you would have been a beggar yourself. God is bountiful to you, not in accordance with your merits, and you yourself wish that he should be bountiful. Why then, having plenty, do you not wish to be generous yourself to your brethren?

It is, however, just that those who work well should enjoy abundance, and that the idle should endure poverty and misery. Therefore, if we know that some are poor only through their own idleness, with such we are not obliged to share the abundance earned by our labour. *If any will not work,* says the apostle Paul, *neither should he eat.*

If you enjoy earthly blessings in full measure, and if you give to the needy, but indulge yourself still more, it means that you do good works without the least self-denial. Your works of charity are not great.

Love for God and our neighbour, in our present corrupt state, is impossible without self-sacrifice; he who wishes to fulfil the commandment ought to devote himself in good time to great deeds and sufferings for the sake of those that he loves.

And he was sad at that saying, and he went away grieved; for he had great possessions. We too are often saddened, weakened, in heart and body, at a single word asking a sacrifice for the sake of the heavenly kingdom, although we were brave enough before.

Bear in your heart continually the words *Christ is love,* and endeavour to love all, sacrificing for the sake of love not only that which you possess, but yourself also.

He truly bestows charity who gives from his heart, who gives lovingly. He is truly merciful who converses with every one from his heart, and not only with the mind and the lips; who renders sincere, heartfelt respect to everyone; who preaches the word of God and serves God with a true heart, and not hypocritically—in a word, who embraces all, and bears all in his heart by love, despite everything of this world that may become a hindrance to love between himself and his neighbour; such a one is truly merciful.

Those who give bread or money to the hungry regretfully, with an evil eye and a discontented heart, act just as if they were poisoning their bread or their alms, though the poison is a spiritual and invisible one. We must give lovingly, with a respect for the person of our neighbour, willingly and gladly; for it is natural that love should rejoice when affording help to the beloved.

Worthless is the charity of the man who bestows it unwillingly because the matter of charity is not his, but the gift of God; only the disposition of his heart belongs to him.

All offerings and charity to the poor will not replace love for our neighbour, if there is no love in the heart; therefore, in bestowing charity, we must be careful that it should be bestowed lovingly, from a sincere heart, willingly and not with a feeling of annoyance. The very word *charity* shows that it should be an act of the heart, and should be bestowed with pity for those in need, and with a feeling of sorrow for our sins, to cleanse which the charity is bestowed; *for alms . . . shall purge away all sin*. He who bestows charity unwillingly does not recognise his sins, has not learned to know himself. Charity is, first of all, a benefit to those who bestow it.

That man is of a noble and elevated spirit who mercifully and generously scatters his gifts upon all, and is glad when he has an opportunity of benefitting and giving pleasure to others without thinking of a reward. That man is of a noble and elevated spirit who is never condescending and haughty towards those who seek him and partake of his bounty, does not neglect them in any respect, does not underrate them in any degree in his thoughts, but esteems them as he esteemed them when he first met them, or higher. As it is, it often happens that we grow condescending towards those who have become ours, and having become accustomed to them, speedily grow tired of them, and reckon them as nothing; we often place a man below a beloved animal or even a beloved object.

It is well in every respect to give to the poor, not only in order to get mercy on the terrible day of judgment. Even here on earth those who give alms often get great mercy from others, and that for which others have to pay large sums of money is given to them freely. Indeed, will not the Lover of mankind, the righteous and bountiful heavenly Father, whose children are lovingly helped by the merciful, reward them here also, in order to encourage them to still greater works of mercy, as well as to cause the unmerciful, who mock at them, to amend? He will reward them both worthily and righteously.

Envy is madness for a Christian. In Christ we are all given infinitely great blessings; are all made godly; are all made inheritors of the kingdom of heaven. And we are also promised enough earthly blessings, provided we seek the righteousness of God and his kingdom. *Seek ye first the kingdom of God and his righteousness, and all these things shall be added unto you.* And we are commanded to be contented with what we have, and not to be covetous.

When your heart is struck with avarice, say to yourself: 'My life is Christ the beloved; he is my inexhaustible wealth, food and drink.' Our blind flesh dreams of finding life in food and in money, and bears ill will towards those who deprive it of them. But be firmly persuaded that your life consists not in money and food, but in mutual love for the sake of love, the love of God.

FIVE

The Ordering of the Daily Life

Remember that the realm of thought and word belongs to God, as well as the whole universe, visible and invisible. You have nothing of your own—not even a word, not even a thought. Everything is God's. Mingle with the common order of things, as nature itself forms one ordered whole. Do not lead a self-loving, separate life.

As you have received everything from God, be ready to give everything back to God, so that having been found faithful in small things you may afterwards be made ruler over many things.

Take the trouble to spend a single day according to God's commandments, and you will see and feel for yourself how good it is to fulfil God's will, which for us is life, eternal blessedness.

You care for the opinion of men, for human glory; set yourself actively to heal this infirmity of your heart. Think and care only for the glory of God. Consider human dishonour as nothing. When you ought to honour a poor or uneducated or uncultured father, or mother, or relation, or friend, or acquaintance, before distinguished and educated men of this world, or to defend any truth in a community that scoffs at it, then regard God alone and his commandments, and be steadfast in your respect for them without cowardice and shame; and the same with regard to standing up for God's truth.

There is no need to ask if we ought to spread or propagate the glory of God, whether by writing, or by word of mouth, or by good works. This is something we are obliged to do according to our ability and opportunity. We must make use of our talents. If you think much about something so clear and simple then perhaps the Devil may suggest to you some such foolishness as that you need only be inwardly active!

Labour and activity are indispensable for all. Life without activity is not life at all, but something monstrous—a ghostly parody of life. That is why it is the duty of every man continually and persistently to combat the slothfulness of the flesh. God preserve every Christian from indulging it!

Strive by every means constantly to delight the heavenly Father by your life; that is, by your meekness, humility, gentleness, obedience, abstinence, right judgment, love of peace, patience, mercy, sincere friendship with worthy people, kindness to everybody, warm hospitality, straight dealing in business, simplicity of heart and character, and purity of thought.

Watch your vices, above all at home, where they appear freely, like moles in a safe place. Outside our own home, some of our vices are usually screened by other more decorous ones, whilst at home there is no possibility of concealing these black moles that undermine the integrity of the soul.

Speak and do all that is right undoubtingly, boldly, firmly and decidedly. Be not doubtful, timid, weak, hesitant, undecided. *For God hath not given us the spirit of fear, but of power and of love.* Our God is a God of power.

Unfortunate is he who loves haste; he will meet with a multitude of annoying obstacles, and he will fume inwardly; through his desire for haste he will be irritated time without number.

Idle talk, or amusement with trifles when you have guests, deprives the heart of faith, of the fear of God, and of love for God. Guests are a scourge to a devout heart. Of course, you must understand that I refer only to such guests as occupy themselves with trifles. Serious, religiously minded guests are very different.

It may happen that there is much wickedness in your soul. But let it be known to God alone, who knows everything, both that which is open, and that which is secret and concealed, and do not show all your uncleanness to others; do not corrupt them by the breath of wickedness concealed within you. Tell God that your soul is full of wickedness, and that your life is near to hell; declare your soul's sickness to your confessor, or to a true and close friend, so that they may teach and direct you; but to other people show a bright and pleasant countenance.

SIX

The Practice of the Presence of God in Daily Life

Believe that God sees you as undoubtingly as you believe that anyone standing face to face with you sees you, only with this difference, that the heavenly Father sees *everything* that is in you, everything that you are.

The Lord is near unto all men, but men themselves are far from him in their hearts, their thoughts, their intentions, and their inclinations, as well as in their words and deeds, which are contrary to the law of God.

When God is present in all a man's thoughts, desires, intentions, words and works, then it means that the kingdom of God has come to him; then he sees God in all things; then the omnipresence of God is most clearly revealed to him, and the true fear of God dwells in his heart; he seeks every moment to please God, and fears every moment lest he sin against God, who is present at his right hand.

In everything, and at every time, strive to please God, and to think of the salvation of your soul from sin and the Devil, and of its adoption by God.

On rising from your bed, make the sign of the cross, and say, *In the Name of the Father, and of the Son, and of the Holy Ghost,* and add, *Vouchsafe, O Lord, to keep us this day without sin, and teach me to do thy will.*

While washing say, *Purge me, O Lord, with hyssop, and I shall be clean; wash me, and I shall be whiter than snow.* When putting on your linen, think of the cleanliness of the heart, and ask it of the Lord, saying *Create in me a clean heart, O God.* If you are putting on new clothes, think of the renewal of the spirit, and say, *Renew a right spirit within me.* Laying aside old clothes with distaste, think with greater distaste of the old, carnal, sinful man, and of laying it also aside.

Tasting the sweetness of bread, think of the true Bread which gives eternal life to the soul, the Body of Christ, and hunger after this Bread—that is, long to partake of it more frequently. In drinking anything, think of the true Drink that quenches the thirst of the soul fevered by vice—the immaculate and lifegiving Blood of Christ.

Resting during the day, think of the eternal rest prepared for those who wrestle and struggle with sin, with the spirits of evil, with human injustice and ignorance. Lying down to sleep at night, think of the sleep of death, which sooner or later will come to all of us; and of that dark, terrible, eternal night into which all impenitent sinners will be cast.

Meeting the day, think of that day that knows no night, eternal, brighter than the brightest earthly day, the day of the kingdom of heaven, when joy shall be bestowed upon all who have striven to please God, or who have repented before God with a whole heart, during this temporal life.

When you go anywhere, think of the righteousness of walking spiritually before God, and say, *Order my steps in thy word, and let no wickedness have dominion over me*. When you do anything, strive to do it thinking of God, the Creator, who has made all things by his infinite wisdom, grace and power, and has created you after his image and likeness.

When you are given any money or goods, think that our inexhaustible treasury, from which we derive all the treasures of soul and body, the ever-flowing source of every blessing, is God; thank him with all your soul, and do not shut up your treasures within yourself, lest you shut the entrance of your heart to the priceless and living treasure—God; but distribute part of your property amongst those that are in want, the poor, the needy; so that upon your brethren in this life you may prove your love and gratitude to God, and for this be rewarded by him in the life to come, which is eternal.

When you see the glitter of silver, be not allured by it, but think how your soul should glitter with Christ's virtues. When you see the glitter of gold, be not allured by it, but remember that your soul ought to be cleansed as gold is, by fire, and that the Lord desires to make you yourself shine like the sun, in the eternal and radiant kingdom of his Father; that there you will behold the Sun of Righteousness, God the Holy Trinity, with the all-holy and ever-virgin Mother of God, and all the angels and saints, filled with unspeakable light, and shining with the light poured upon them.

God is nearer to us than any man at any time. Therefore we must always set God before us, at our right hand, and there behold him; we must be strong, and in order not to sin we must so place ourselves that nothing can thrust God from our thoughts and hearts, that nothing can hide him from us, that nothing may deprive us of our beloved Lord, but that we may every hour, every minute, belong to him, and be perpetually with him, as he himself is perpetually with us, as he constantly cares for us and guards us.

SEVEN

The Proper Use of the Intellect

Truth is the foundation of everything that has been created. Let truth be also the foundation of all your works, inward and outward alike, and—above all—the foundation of your prayers. Let all your life—all your thoughts, all your desires, all your works—be founded upon truth.

How must we look upon the gifts of intellect, feeling and freedom? With the intellect we must learn to know God in the works of his creation, revelation and providence, and in the destinies of men; with the heart we must feel God's love, and heavenly peace, and must love our neighbour, sympathise with him in joy and in sorrow, in health and in sickness, in poverty or in wealth, in high esteem and in low; we must use freedom as a means, as an instrument wherewith to do as much good as possible, and to perfect ourselves in every virtue, that we may render unto God fruits a hundredfold.

Remember that the intellect is the servant of the heart, which is our life; if it leads the heart to truth, peace, joy and life, then it fulfils its purpose, it is true; but if it leads the heart to doubt, disturbance, torment, despondency, darkness, then it does not fulfil its purpose, and is absolutely false—*knowledge, falsely so called.*

210

If the heart feels peace, joy and ease from faith in anything, this is enough; it is not necessary to demand of the reason proofs of the truth of such an object—it is without doubt true, for the heart asserts its truth by its life.

Do not forget yourself in looking upon the beauty of the human face, but look upon the soul; do not look upon the man's garment (the body is his temporary garment), but look upon him who is clothed in it. Do not admire the magnificence of the house, but look upon the man who dwells in it, and what he is; otherwise you will offend the image of God in the man, will dishonour the King by worshipping his servant, and not rendering unto him even the least part of the honour due to him.

When you see a beautiful girl or woman, or a handsome youth or man, lift up your thoughts at once to the supreme most holy beauty, the author of every heavenly and earthly beauty, God himself; glorify him for having created such beauty out of mere earth; marvel at the beauty of God's image in man, which shines forth even in our fallen state; imagine what our image shall be when we shine forth in the kingdom of our Father, if we become worthy of it; picture to yourself what must be the beauty of God's saints, of the holy angels, of the Mother of God herself, adorned with divine glory; imagine the unspeakable goodness of God's countenance, which we shall behold, and be not led astray by merely earthly beauty, by flesh and blood. Merely carnal desire is sweet, but it is corrupting and contrary to God's will. Hold fast to God alone, not to fleeting carnal beauty.

Music: do not be led astray by the melodious sounds of an instrument or a voice; but by their effect upon the soul consider what is their spirit: if the sounds produce within your soul feelings that are calm, chaste, holy, then listen to them, and feed your soul upon them; but if they rouse your soul to lust, or anger, or some other ill-feeling, then cease listening, and throw aside both the flesh and the spirit of such music.

Let all knowledge relating to faith or religion be as though always new to you—that is, having the same importance, interest, holiness.

You wish to comprehend the incomprehensible; but can you understand how the inward sorrows with which your heart is overwhelmed overtake you, and can you find, except in the Lord, the means to drive them away? Learn at first, with your heart, how to free yourself from sorrows, how to ensure peace in your heart, and then, if necessary, philosophise on the incomprehensible, for *if ye then be not able to do that thing which is least, why take ye thought for the rest?*

It is extremely dangerous to develop—to educate—only the understanding, the intellect, and to ignore the heart. We must, above all, attend to the heart, for the heart is life, but life corrupted by sin. It is necessary to purify this source of life, to kindle in it the pure flame of life, so that it may burn, and not go out; so that it may direct all the thoughts, desires, and inclinations of the man throughout his life.

Want of spiritual education, of the development and amendment of the heart, is a thousand times more culpable than want of mental education; for a man intellectually uneducated is in darkness, and deserves indulgence and pity, whilst an educated man given up to his vices, with all his knowledge, and with the knowledge of the will of God, is a man whose heart is hardened, and who is dead to God; for he does not apply the principles he has learned; he does not fulfil the will of

God, but transgresses it with even greater daring and insolence than does the uneducated.

The uneducated man's simplicity of heart, his meekness, gentleness, humility, and unassertive patience, are dearer to God than all our knowledge, all our external polish, all our studied expressions, all our feigned courtesy, all our lengthy prayers, all our artful speeches. Even sins themselves are more excusable in the uneducated, as sins of ignorance. Therefore respect simple want of education, and learn from it what is not possessed by the so-called educated: simplicity, gentleness, patience and other virtues. The uneducated are the babes in Christ, to whom the Lord sometimes reveals his mysteries.

EIGHT

Afflictions

Afflictions are a great teacher; they show us our weaknesses, vices, and need of repentance; they cleanse the soul, and sober it, as from drunkenness; they bring down grace, they soften the hard heart, they inspire us with a loathing for sin, and strengthen us in faith, hope and virtue.

In times of rest, ease and comfort of the flesh, the latter revives, whilst when we are oppressed, vexed or weary, it is subdued; this is why the heavenly Father, in his wisdom and mercy, subjects our soul and body to severe distresses and sicknesses, and why we must not only endure them patiently, but must rejoice in them, even more than in spiritual calm, ease, and bodily health. For the spiritual state of the man who is not subjected to spiritual affliction or bodily sickness must undoubtedly be bad, particularly if he has an abundance of earthly blessings; all kinds of sin and vice are imperceptibly generated in his heart, and he is thus exposed to spiritual death.

If you do not yourself know and suffer the wiles of the evil spirit, you will not know, and will not value as you ought, the benefits bestowed upon you by the Holy Spirit of God. Not knowing the spirit that destroys, you will not know the Spirit that gives life. Only by means of direct contrasts of good and evil, of life and death, can we clearly know and recognise the one and the other. If you are not subjected to distresses, to the danger of bodily or spiritual death, you will not truly know the Lord, the giver of life, who delivers us from these distresses and from eternal death, spiritual death.

Ought not the Christian, who looks for eternal peace and joy in heaven, to bear courageously and joyfully all sorrows, labour, sickness, injustice, everything unpleasant, here? Indeed he ought. Otherwise, what would be the meaning of future rest and peace? What peace and rest shall there be for him who has already had his peace and rest here, without enduring anything? Where would God's justice be? *We must through much tribulation enter into the kingdom of God.*

The true Christian ought to long for outward, carnal, worldly, sufferings, for they strengthen his spirit. He must not even think of murmuring at them. How can he murmur at that which is profitable to his immortal soul, even if the means are very repugnant to his carnal man?

Our flesh becomes depressed and downcast when it is subjected to any infirmity; whilst when it is in good health, and enjoys carnal pleasures, it jumps for joy, and gets beyond itself. We must take no notice of the delusive feelings of the flesh, and, in general, must refuse with contempt every carnal amusement and delight; we must bear with equanimity the troubles and illnesses of the flesh, take courage, and set our trust in God.

Do not despond when sorely tempted, afflicted, or sick, or at obstacles arising from the disturbance of the enemy; all this is the reproof and chastisement of the righteous Lord, to cleanse, arouse and correct you, to burn out the thorns of carnal vices.

Do not complain if sometimes you suffer greatly. Do not think of the suffering, but of the blessed consequences of this chastisement, and the health of the soul. What would you not do for the health of your body? Still more must you bear everything for the health and salvation of your soul which lives eternally.

Thy will be done. For instance, when you wish, and by every means endeavour, to be well and healthy, and yet remain ill, then say, *Thy will be done*. When you undertake something, and your undertaking does not succeed, say *Thy will be done*. When you do good to others, and they repay you with evil, say, *Thy will be done*. Or when you wish to sleep, and cannot, say, *Thy will be done*. In general, do not be irritated when something is not done in accordance with *your* will, but learn to submit in everything to the will of your heavenly Father. You would not like to be tempted, and yet every day the enemy harasses you, provokes and annoys you by every possible means. Do not become irritated and angered, but say, *Thy will be done*.

It is never so difficult to say from the heart *Thy will be done,* as when we are sorely afflicted or gravely ill, and above all when we are subjected to the injustice of men, or the assaults and wiles of the enemy. It is also difficult to say it from the heart when we are ourselves the cause of some misfortune, for then we think that it is not God's will, but our own will, that has reduced us to this state, although nothing can in fact happen except by the will of God.

It is difficult sincerely to believe that it is the will of God that we should suffer, when the heart knows both by faith and experience that God is our blessedness; and, therefore it is difficult to say in misfortune, *Thy will be done.* But when it is difficult for our corrupt nature to acknowledge the will of God over us, that will of God without which nothing happens, and humbly to submit to it, that is the very time humbly to submit to it, and to offer to the Lord our most precious sacrifice —heartfelt devotion, not only in the time of ease and happiness, but also in suffering and misfortune. It is then that we must submit our vain and erring wisdom to the perfect wisdom of God, for the thoughts of God are as far from our thoughts *as the heavens are higher than the earth.*

God tests the several sinful attachments of our hearts in different ways, in order to disclose to each the weak, diseased parts of his heart, and to teach each one of us to correct himself. In many, a sword shall pierce through their own soul, that the thoughts of their hearts may be revealed.

Do not fear the conflict, do not flee it; where there is no struggle, there is no virtue; where faith and love are not tempted, one cannot be sure whether they really exist. They are proved and revealed in adversity, that is, in difficult and grievous circumstances, external or internal, in sickness, sorrow and privations.

Many say that they believe in God; but should any misfortune or temptation arise, they grow faint-hearted and despondent. Sometimes they begin to murmur. And what becomes of all their faith? This should be the very time to submit to the will of God, and to bless the name of the Lord. Otherwise it is evident that they only believe in God in the time of happiness, and renounce him in the time of misfortune.

Unwillingly, faint-heartedly, with murmurings and blasphemy against the Lord, we bear the cruel afflictions of our heart, not seeing the profit which should be derived from bearing them patiently and submissively. We do not wish to see that our heart has waxed gross, and become infected by various vices; that it is proud, cunning, malicious and adulterous, and cleaves to earthly things; and that it cannot be cleansed and made humble, and become good, and submissive to God, except it be cruelly afflicted and greatly oppressed.

NINE

Sickness

When your flesh suffers through illness, remember that it is the greatest enemy of your salvation that suffers, that is weakened by these sufferings, and bear them bravely in the name of the Lord Jesus Christ, who for our sakes endured the cross and suffered death; also remember that all our illnesses are God's punishment for sins; they cleanse us, they reconcile us to God, and lead us back to his love.

In our eyes, illnesses appear only as painful, unpleasant, indeed terrible. It is seldom that any one of us during the time of sickness represents to himself the profit which his illness brings to his soul; but in God's all-wise and most merciful providence, not a single illness remains without some profit to our soul. Sickness in the hand of providence is as a bitter medicine for the soul, curing its vices, its bad habits, its evil desires. Not a single sickness sent to us shall return void. We must keep in mind the usefulness of illnesses, that we may bear them more easily and more calmly.

You are ill, and your illness is very painful; you are low-spirited and despondent; you are troubled and tossed with thoughts, each darker than the last; your heart and your lips are ready to murmur, to blaspheme God. Listen to my sincere advice. Bear your illness bravely, and do not merely not despond, but on the contrary rejoice, if you can, in your illness. You would ask me what there is for you to rejoice at when you are racked all over with pain? Rejoice that the Lord has sent you this temporary chastisement, in order to cleanse your soul from sins. *For whom the Lord loveth he chasteneth.*

When you are ill, rejoice in the fact that you are not gratifying those vices which you would have been gratifying had you been in good health; rejoice that you are bearing the cross of sickness and that therefore you are treading the narrow and sorrowful way leading to the kingdom of heaven.

218

Remember that during your illness the Lord himself is with you—*I am with him in trouble*—and that it has proceeded as a sign of the Master, punishing us as a Father. You who believe when you are well, see to it that you do not fall away from God in the time of misfortune, but, like the martyrs, be constant in faith, hope and love.

You ask the Lord that you may love him with a love, strong as death, or until death. Suppose now that the Lord sends you a terrible disease that may bring you nigh unto death itself. Do not then murmur, but bear it bravely, thanking the Lord, and this will show that what you call your love for God *is* strong as death. And during the worst spasms of your illness trust in God, that he has the power to save you, not only from suffering, but even from death itself, should it please him to do so.

When, owing to sickness, you feel unwell and indisposed, and your prayer is cold, heavy, filled with despondency, do not be disheartened, do not despair, for the Lord knows that you are sick. Struggle against your illness, pray as much as you have strength to, and the Lord will not despise the infirmity of your flesh and spirit.

In sickness and affliction, and during bodily infirmity in general, a man cannot in the beginning burn with faith and love for God, because in sickness and affliction the heart aches, whilst faith and love require a sound heart, a calm heart. This is why we must not very much grieve if during sickness and affliction we cannot believe in God, love him, or pray to him, as fervently as we ought.

Make us glad according to the days wherein thou hast afflicted us, and the years wherein we have seen evil. The merciful

Lord, having punished us, forgives us afterwards by his temporal and eternal mercy. Sometimes a sick person suffers a long while from his illness, as from a wicked tyrant; but during this illness his soul is purified like gold; he obtains the freedom of the children of God, and is deemed worthy of eternal peace and blessedness.

XII

THE LAST THINGS

ONE

Death

What is most terrible to man? Death? Yes, death. None of us can imagine without terror how he will have to breathe his last. But brethren, do not fear, and do not sorrow beyond measure. By his death Jesus Christ has conquered our death, and by his resurrection he has laid the foundation for our resurrection. Every week, every Sunday, we solemnise in the risen Christ our common future resurrection from the dead, and begin beforehand the life eternal, to which this present temporal life is but a short, narrow and most sorrowful way.

For a true Christian, death is but a sleep until the day of resurrection, or a birth into a new life. And in solemnising every week the resurrection of Christ, and with it our own resurrection from the dead, let us learn continually to die to sin, and to rise with our souls from dead works, to enrich ourselves with virtues, and not to sorrow inconsolably for the dead. Let us learn to meet death without dread, as the decree of the heavenly Father, which, through the resurrection of Christ from the dead, has lost its terror.

Sometimes when greatly afflicted you wish to die. It is easy to die—it does not take long; but are you prepared for death? Remember that after death the judgment of your whole life will follow. You are not prepared for death, and if it were to come to you, you would shudder all over. Therefore do not waste words. Do not say that it is better to die; rather, ask how you can prepare for death in a Christian manner. By means of faith, by means of good works, and by bravely bearing whatever happens to you, so that you may be able to meet death fearlessly, peacefully, and without shame, not as a rigorous law of nature, but as a fatherly call of the eternal, heavenly, holy and blessed Father unto the everlasting kingdom.

For man the earthly life, life in the body, serves only to prepare us for life eternal, which will begin after the death of the body. Therefore we must, without delay, make use of this present life to prepare ourselves for that other life to come; and as on week-days we work for this life, so on Sundays and other holy days we must work wholly for the Lord our God.

A true Christian so behaves in this life that it may prepare him for the life to come. He does not think what will be said of his deeds here, but of what will be said in heaven; he represents to himself that he is always in the presence of God, of the angels and of the saints, and bears in mind that one day they will bear witness of his thoughts, words and deeds.

They sin greatly who neglect to educate themselves spiritually for eternal life in the age to come. How can we forget our final destiny? How is it possible to be so ungrateful to the Creator, who created us after his own image and likeness, incorruptible, and for union with himself; who redeemed us by his cross, and opened to us the gates of the kingdom of heaven? How is it that many of us become *like unto the beasts that perish? Let us lift up our hearts!*

A terrible truth. Impenitent sinners after death lose every possibility of changing for good, and therefore are unalterably given up to everlasting torments (for sin cannot but torment). This is proved by the actual state of some sinners, and by the nature of sin itself—to keep the man its prisoner, and to close every way of escape.

But for the grace of God, what sinner would have returned to God? For it is the nature of sin to darken our souls and to bind us hand and foot. But the time and place for grace to act is here alone: after death there are but the prayers of the Church, and these prayers are effective only for penitent sinners—that is, only for those who are able to accept God's mercy, able to benefit by the prayers of the Church, by the light of the good works which they have taken with them out of this life. Impenitent sinners are undoubtedly lost.

TWO

Eternal Life in God

A day is the symbol of the transitory character of this earthly life; noon comes soon upon morning, and is followed by evening, and with the coming of night the whole day has passed away. So does life itself pass away. First childhood, like early morning; then adolescence and manhood, like full day and noon; and lastly old age, if God grants it; afterwards, inevitably, death.

Look upon everything in this world as upon a fleeting shadow and cling with your heart to nothing of it; consider nothing in this world great, and lay your hopes upon nothing earthly. Cling to the one eternal, invisible, only wise God. *We look not at the things which are seen, but at the things which are not seen; for the things which are seen are temporal, but the things which are not seen are eternal.*

That to which a man turns, that which he loves—that he will find. If he loves earthly things, he will find earthly things, and these earthly things will abide in his heart, will communicate their own earthiness to him, and will find him; if he loves heavenly things, he will find heavenly things, and they will abide in his heart, and give him life.

What is the sign that a man is near to Christ? The man who is near to Christ often turns to him with faith and love; often pronounces his most sweet name; often calls upon him for help; often turns his eyes, thoughts and heart towards him. Christ the Lord naturally reveals himself upon his lips and in his glance, because without Christ he is powerless, joyless.

The man who is far from Christ seldom, very seldom, turns his thoughts towards Christ, and even then not with heartfelt faith and love, but only through some necessity, and as to a person who is little known to him, in whom he has no delight, and who in no way attracts him.

Those who are near to Christ ever bear him in mind and heart; they live in him; to them he is breath, food, drink, dwelling—everything. *My soul hangeth upon thee.* And in this they find unspeakable bliss, such as the world does not know. Such are the signs by which it may be recognised who has found Christ.

226

Those who have not found Christ live in this world without hearty faith; they think and care rather about wordly things; and so they go on, while time flees away, until at last the terrible hour comes in which their course is finished, and their time is lost, when the power of their sins will fall upon them, and crush them eternally.

Even here I rest in Christ and with Christ; how, then, can I do otherwise than believe that eternal rest in him awaits me after death, after the struggle against earthly enemies? Here without Christ I feel oppressed and in pain; how can I do otherwise than believe that it will be yet more grievous to be without Christ there, when he will finally cast me away from before his face? Thus the present state of our soul foreshadows the future, which will be a continuation of the present inward state, only in a different degree; for the righteous it will be turned into the fulness of eternal glory; for sinners, into the fulness of everlasting torment.

That our union with God in the future world will indeed come about, and that it will be for us the source of light, peace, joy and bliss; this we partly recognise by experience even in the present life. During prayer, when our soul is wholly turned towards God, and is united to him, we feel happy, calm, easy, joyful, like children resting on their mother's breast; rather, I would say, we experience an inexpressible well-being. *It is good for us to be here.*

As God is the ever-flowing source, we have only to be united to him by lively faith and love unfeigned in order to be filled by him with every spiritual blessing. Such union is possible at every time and in every place, if only our hearts are ever with him, and not with the Devil and the vanity of this world. This is why amongst righteous men we often find seers and prophets working miracles of divine omnipotence, love and mercy—steadfast, unchangeable in virtue unto the laying down of their lives for the faith, out of love for God, and filled with spiritual wisdom, *for the Lord their God is holy*.

As your thought is near to you, as your faith is near to you, so is God near to you, and the more lively and steadfast is your thought about God, the more lively and steadfast your faith, and the recognition of your weakness, your nothingness, and of your need for God, the nearer will God be to you. You cannot live for a single moment without God, and you actually live each moment in him: *For in him we live, and move, and have our being*.

He that is joined unto the Lord through the prayer of faith and the works of love *is one spirit* with the Lord, and therefore he is filled, according to the measure of his faith and love, with wisdom and spiritual power; he receives from him, as from the true goodness, all things leading to salvation, and himself becomes merciful and compassionate to others, is filled with spiritual wisdom, and established in faith and virtue.

The problem of our life is to unite ourselves with God, and sin completely prevents this; therefore flee from sin as from a terrible enemy, as from the destroyer of the soul, because to be without God is death. Let us therefore understand our destiny; let us always remember that our common Master calls us to union with himself.

Struggle unremittingly for everlasting bliss, the beginning of which you know by experience even in the present life; but bear in mind that these beginnings are only earthly, imperfect, which we see now only in part, as *through a glass darkly*. How will it be with us then, when we shall indeed be most truly united to God, when the images and shadows shall pass away, and the kingdom of truth and sight shall come?

God is all-perfect, and you too, according to your receptivity, according to your faith and love, will be made a partaker of his divine perfection. In the union of your soul with God, do not think anything impossible or difficult of fulfilment, *for with God all things are possible*—not only the things you can, or do, think of, but also those of which you cannot think, or which you think of as impossible.

Now we rise and fall, in faith and virtue, but we hope for a time and a state when we shall no longer fall, when we shall reach a state such as that of the angels, who are now inaccessible to evil, and when we shall be established in holiness. In the meantime fight against sin, and hope that at last the time will come of perfect victory over sin, and over death the offspring of sin. *The last enemy that shall be destroyed is death.*

Now we seek lasting bliss, and do not find it. The pleasures which we invent do not last; they are false, empty, and endure but a short time; but if the Christian walks worthy of his calling, then shall he inherit a bliss which is true and lasting, and which shall completely satisfy his soul.

The unspeakable bliss of them that behold the infinite goodness of thy countenance. All earthly bliss passes away, of itself, and through the vicissitudes of life; whilst the joys of heavenly bliss will never end, never pass away. Is it not then worth while to despise all the enjoyments of this transitory world, and of this still more fleeting life, in order to strive with the whole heart after spiritual and abiding joys?

All present things are but a shadow of the future. Present light, for example, is a shadow of light ineffable. Earthly bliss is a pale shadow of that future bliss which is unspeakable and eternal; fire a pale shadow of the fire of Gehenna, which will burn sinners throughout all ages; pure earthly joy a shadow of future joys indescribable.

The degrees of bliss and torment in the next world will vary. This is proved by the present state of the souls of different people, or of the same man at different times, in different circumstances. The simpler, the better and more unselfish a man is, the more blessed he is inwardly; the more dishonest, selfish and evil he is, the more unhappy; the firmer his faith and the stronger his love, the more blessed he is; the weaker his faith and love, the weaker he feels. Thus, those who have little or no faith, those who hate their fellows, are the most unhappy of men. By this we can understand what future torments will be, and future bliss.